ARTHUR MILLER

CORNELSEN SENIOR ENGLISH LIBRARY

The Crucible

Cornelsen

Arthur Miller ***The Crucible***

Herausgegeben von:
Anne Herlyn

Verlagsredaktion:
Ralph Williams, Christine Finke (Assistenz)

Umschlaggestaltung:
Cornelsen Schulverlage Design; *Bildrecherche*: Josephine Wolff

Umschlagfoto:
© Diane Seddon Photography / Flickr Open / Getty Images

Typografie:
Annika Preyhs für Buchgestaltung+

Technische Umsetzung:
Britta Dieterle, Buch und Gestaltung

www.cornelsen.de

1. Auflage, 3. Druck 2014

Alle Drucke dieser Auflage sind inhaltlich unverändert
und können im Unterricht nebeneinander verwendet werden.

Druck: Offizin Andersen Nexö Leipzig

ISBN 978-3-06-033442-1

Inhalt gedruckt auf säurefreiem Papier aus nachhaltiger Forstwirtschaft.

CONTENTS

For Mary

Abbreviations and Annotations

adj	adjective	**fml**	formal
adv	adverb	**infml**	informal
AE	American English	**jdm./jdn.**	jemandem/en
ca.	circa; about	**Lat.**	Latin
cf.	confer; see	**n**	noun
derog.	derogatory	**sb.**	somebody
e.g.	exempli gratia; for example	**sl**	slang
esp.	especially	**sth.**	something
etc.	et cetera; and so on	**usu.**	usually
fig.	figurative	**v**	verb

The annotations are arranged chronologically; the first time a word is used is where you will find it explained.

A Play in Four Acts

A note on the historical accuracy of this play

This play is not history in the sense in which the word is used by the academic historian. Dramatic purposes have sometimes required many characters to be fused into one; the number of girls involved in the 'crying-out' has been reduced; Abigail's age has been raised; while there were several judges of almost equal authority, I have symbolized them all in Hathorne and Danforth. However, I believe that the reader will discover here the essential nature of one of the strangest and most awful chapters in human history. The fate of each character is exactly that of his historical model, and there is no one in the drama who did not play a similar – and in some cases exactly the same – role in history.

As for the characters of the persons, little is known about most of them excepting what may be surmised from a few letters, the trial record, certain broadsides written at the time, and references to their conduct in sources of varying reliability. They may therefore be taken as creations of my own, drawn to the best of my ability in conformity with their known behaviour, except as indicated in the commentary I have written for this text.

2 **historian**: person who has studied history 2–3 **require sth. to be done**: need sth. to be done 3 **fuse into one**: combine (two or more items) so they become one 3–4 **be involved in sth.**: be part of sth. 4 **crying-out**: (here) accusations 5 **authority**: (here) rank 6 **symbolize**: stand for 13 **surmise**: guess 13–14 **trial record**: written documentation of a court trial (*Gerichtsverhandlung*) 14 **broadside** ['brɔːdsaɪd]: *Flugblatt* 15 **conduct** (n) [kən'dʌkt]: the way a person behaves 16–17 **in conformity with sth.**: *in Übereinstimmung mit etw.*

Characters

(in order of appearance)

REVEREND PARRIS

BETTY PARRIS

TITUBA

ABIGAIL WILLIAMS

SUSANNA WALCOTT

ANN PUTNAM

THOMAS PUTNAM

MERCY LEWIS

MARY WARREN

JOHN PROCTOR

REBECCA NURSE

GILES COREY

REVEREND JOHN HALE

ELIZABETH PROCTOR

FRANCIS NURSE

EZEKIEL CHEEVER

MARSHAL HERRICK

JUDGE HATHORNE

DEPUTY-GOVERNOR DANFORTH

SARAH GOOD

HOPKINS

ACT ONE

(AN OVERTURE)

A small upper bedroom in the home of REVEREND SAMUEL PARRIS, *Salem, Massachusetts, in the spring of the year 1692.*

There is a narrow window at the left. Through its leaded panes the morning sunlight streams. A candle still burns near the bed, which is at the right. A chest, a chair, and a small table are the other furnishings. At the back a door opens on the landing of the stairway to the ground floor. The room gives off an air of clean spareness. The roof rafters are exposed, and the wood colours are raw and unmellowed.

As the curtain rises, REVEREND PARRIS *is discovered kneeling beside the bed, evidently in prayer. His daughter,* BETTY PARRIS, *aged ten, is lying on the bed, inert.*

At the time of these events Parris was in his middle forties. In history he cut a villainous path, and there is very little good to be said for him. He believed he was being persecuted wherever he went, despite his best efforts to win people and God to his side. In meeting, he felt insulted if someone rose to shut the door without first asking his permission. He was a widower with no interest in children, or talent with them. He regarded them as young adults, and until this strange crisis he, like the rest of Salem, never conceived that the children were anything but thankful for being permitted to walk straight,

overture ['əʊvətʃʊə(r)]: introduction (normally to a piece of music) 2 **Salem** ['seɪləm]: small city in Massachusetts (Northeast U.S.) 3 **leaded panes** ['ledɪd]: pieces of glass connected by thin strips of lead to form a window 4 **stream** (v): flow 5 **furnishings**: objects in a room 6 **landing**: platform at the top of a flight of stairs 7 **spareness**: simplicity **rafter**: thick beam of wood that holds up the roof **exposed**: visible 8 **raw**: natural **unmellowed**: left in a rough natural state 9 **kneel**: be in a position close to the ground where your body rests on your knees 11 **inert** [ɪ'nɜːt]: not moving 13 **cut a villainous path** ['vɪlənəs]: go in the direction of evil 14 **persecute sb.**: treat sb. very badly because of their race, religion, etc. 15 **meeting**: (here) religious gathering 17 **widower**: man whose wife has died 19 **conceive**: imagine eyes slightly lowered, arms at the sides, and mouths shut until bidden to speak.

His house stood in the 'town' – but we today would hardly call it a village. The meeting house was near by, and from this point outward – toward the bay or inland – there were a few small-windowed, dark houses snuggling against the raw Massachusetts winter. Salem had been established hardly forty years before. To the European world the whole province was a barbaric frontier inhabited by a sect of fanatics who, nevertheless, were shipping out products of slowly increasing quantity and value.

No one can really know what their lives were like. They had no novelists – and would not have permitted anyone to read a novel if one were handy. Their creed forbade anything resembling a theatre or 'vain enjoyment'. They did not celebrate Christmas, and a holiday from work meant only that they must concentrate even more upon prayer.

Which is not to say that nothing broke into this strict and sombre way of life. When a new farmhouse was built, friends assembled to 'raise the roof', and there would be special foods cooked and probably some potent cider passed around. There was a good supply of ne'er-do-wells in Salem, who dallied at the shovelboard in Bridget Bishop's tavern. Probably more than the creed, hard work kept the morals of the place from spoiling, for the people were forced to fight the land like heroes for every grain of corn, and no man had very much time for fooling around.

That there were some jokers, however, is indicated by the practice of appointing a two-man patrol whose duty was to 'walk forth in the time of God's worship to take notice of such as either lye about the

2 **bid sb. to do sth.**: ask sb. to do sth. 4 **meeting house**: place where the Puritans met to pray 6 **snuggle**: rest comfortably 7 **establish sth.**: start sth. 8 **frontier** **['frʌntɪə(r)]**: the edge *(Rand)* of civilization 13 **creed**: statement of religious beliefs 14 **vain**: for no good reason 17 **sombre**: serious 18 **assemble**: get together 19 **raise the roof**: (here) celebrate 20 **potent cider**: strong alcoholic drink made from apples 21 **ne'er-do-well [neə(r) də wel]**: badly behaved person **dally**: (old-fashioned) hang around and waste time **shovelboard**: old form of billiard played on the ground 25 **fool around**: do annoying things 27 **walk forth** (old use): walk around 28 **lye about** (old use): hang around

meeting house, without attending to the word and ordinances, or that lye at home or in the fields without giving good account thereof, and to take the names of such persons, and to present them to the magistrates, whereby they may be accordingly proceeded against'. This predilection for minding other people's business was time-honoured among the people of Salem, and it undoubtedly created many of the suspicions which were to feed the coming madness. It was also, in my opinion, one of the things that a John Proctor would rebel against, for the time of the armed camp had almost passed, and since the country was reasonably – although not wholly – safe, the old disciplines were beginning to rankle. But, as in all such matters, the issue was not clear-cut, for danger was still a possibility, and in unity still lay the best promise of safety.

The edge of the wilderness was close by. The American continent stretched endlessly west, and it was full of mystery for them. It stood, dark and threatening, over their shoulders night and day, for out of it Indian tribes marauded from time to time, and Reverend Parris had parishioners who had lost relatives to these heathen.

The parochial snobbery of these people was partly responsible for their failure to convert the Indians. Probably they also preferred to take land from heathens rather than from fellow Christians. At any rate, very few Indians were converted, and the Salem folk believed that the virgin forest was the Devil's last preserve, his home base and

1 **attend to sth.** (old-fashioned): pay attention to sth. **ordinance** (old use): religious ceremony 2 **give account of sth.** (old use): justify *(rechtfertigen)* a certain action 4 **magistrate** (old use): person who makes sure that laws are obeyed **accordingly**: *angemessen* **proceed against sb.**: deal with sb. who has done sth. wrong 5 **predilection for sth.**: liking for sth. **mind other people's business**: be interested in other peoples' private lives 5–6 **time-honoured**: liked because it has existed for a long time 7 **suspicion**: idea or feeling that someone has done sth. wrong 11 **discipline**: set of rules **rankle**: (here) make people angry 17 **maraud** **[mə'rɔːd]**: move around in search of sth. to destroy or steal 18 **parishioner** **[pə'rɪʃənə(r)]**: member of a church community **heathen ['hiːðn]**: term used by religious people to refer to those who with a different religion or no religion 19 **parochial snobbery [pə'rəʊkiəl]**: thinking you are better than others because of your faith 21 **fellow** (adj): members of the same group as you 23 **virgin forest**: forest that is still in its original, natural state **preserve** (n): place just for you

the citadel of his final stand. To the best of their knowledge the American forest was the last place on earth that was not paying homage to God.

For these reasons, among others, they carried about an air of innate resistance, even of persecution. Their fathers had, of course, been persecuted in England. So now they and their church found it necessary to deny any other sect its freedom, lest their New Jerusalem be defiled and corrupted by wrong ways and deceitful ideas.

They believed, in short, that they held in their steady hands the candle that would light the world. We have inherited this belief, and it has helped and hurt us. It helped them with the discipline it gave them. They were a dedicated folk, by and large, and they had to be to survive the life they had chosen or been born into in this country.

The proof of their belief's value to them may be taken from the opposite character of the first Jamestown settlement, farther south, in Virginia. The Englishmen who landed there were motivated mainly by a hunt for profit. They had thought to pick off the wealth of the new country and then return rich to England. They were a band of individualists, and a much more ingratiating group than the Massachusetts men. But Virginia destroyed them. Massachusetts tried to kill off the Puritans, but they combined; they set up a communal society which, in the beginning, was little more than an armed camp with an autocratic and very devoted leadership. It was, however, an autocracy by consent, for they were united from top to bottom by a commonly held ideology whose perpetuation was the reason and justification for all their sufferings. So their self-denial, their purposefulness, their suspicion of all vain pursuits, their hard-

1 **citadel**: castle where townspeople could go for protection during an attack **final stand**: ultimate act of defense 2–3 **pay homage to sb.**: ['hɒmɪdʒ] honour sb. 5 **innate [ɪ'neɪt]**: that you were born with 7 **lest**: in case 8 **defile**: ruin **corrupt**: spoil 12 **dedicated**: willing to work hard 19 **ingratiating**: acting pleasant in order to please others 22 **communal society**: society in which members work closely together 23 **autocratic**: with absolute power in ruling a community 24 **devoted**: loyal **autocracy [ɔː'tɒkrəsi]**: a system with an autocratic leader 25 **perpetuation [pəˌpetʃu'eɪʃn]**: (here) survival 26 **self-denial [self dɪ'naɪəl]**: not allowing yourself sth. you enjoy 27 **vain pursuit [pə'sjuːt]**: activity that is considered a waste of time

handed justice, were altogether perfect instruments for the conquest of this space so antagonistic to man.

But the people of Salem in 1691 were not quite the dedicated folk that arrived on the *Mayflower*. A vast differentiation had taken place, and in their own time a revolution had unseated the royal government and substituted a junta which was at this moment in power. The times, to their eyes, must have been out of joint, and to the common folk must have seemed as insoluble and complicated as do ours today. It is not hard to see how easily many could have been led to believe that the time of confusion had been brought upon them by deep and darkling forces. No hint of such speculation appears on the court record, but social disorder in any age breeds such mystical suspicions, and when, as in Salem, wonders are brought forth from below the social surface, it is too much to expect people to hold back very long from laying on the victims with all the force of their frustrations.

The Salem tragedy, which is about to begin in these pages, developed from a paradox. It is a paradox in whose grip we still live, and there is no prospect yet that we will discover its resolution. Simply, it was this: for good purposes, even high purposes, the people of Salem developed a theocracy, a combine of state and religious power whose function was to keep the community together, and to prevent any kind of disunity that might open it to destruction by material or ideological enemies. It was forged for a necessary purpose and accomplished that purpose. But all organization is and must be grounded on the idea of exclusion and prohibition, just as two objects cannot occupy the same space. Evidently the time came

1 **hard-handed**: strict **conquest**: act of taking control of a place, usu. by force 2 **antagonistic**: hostile 5 **unseat sb.**: take away power from sb. (e.g. a ruler) 6 **junta** [ˈdʒʌntə]: military government that used force to gain power 7 **out of joint**: not working in a normal way 8 **insoluble** [ɪnˈsɒljəbl]: impossible to solve 11 **darkling** (literary): dark 12 **court record**: official document of a trial 15 **lay on sb.**: attack sb. 16 **frustration**: disappointment 19 **prospect**: chance 21 **theocracy** [θiˈɒkrəsi]: a government that is ruled by religious leaders **combine** (old use): combination 23 **disunity**: not agreeing with each other 24 **forge**: create with great effort 25 **accomplish**: achieve 26 **exclusion**: not letting people be part of a group or enter a place **prohibition**: ban

in New England when the repressions of order were heavier than seemed warranted by the dangers against which the order was organized. The witch-hunt was a perverse manifestation of the panic which set in among all classes when the balance began to turn toward greater individual freedom.

When one rises above the individual villainy displayed, one can only pity them all, just as we shall be pitied some day. It is still impossible for man to organize his social life without repressions, and the balance has yet to be struck between order and freedom.

The witch-hunt was not, however, a mere repression. It was also, and as importantly, a long overdue opportunity for everyone so inclined to express publicly his guilt and sins, under the cover of accusations against the victims. It suddenly became possible – and patriotic and holy – for a man to say that Martha Corey had come into his bedroom at night, and that, while his wife was sleeping at his side, Martha laid herself down on his chest and 'nearly suffocated him'. Of course it was her spirit only, but his satisfaction at confessing himself was no lighter than if it had been Martha herself. One could not ordinarily speak such things in public.

Long-held hatreds of neighbours could now be openly expressed, and vengeance taken, despite the Bible's charitable injunctions. Land-lust which had been expressed before by constant bickering over boundaries and deeds, could now be elevated to the arena of morality; one could cry witch against one's neighbour and feel

1 **repression**: strict control of a group of people 2 **warranted**: necessary
4 **witch-hunt**: persecution of those who are thought to be controlled by the devil
manifestation: visible sign 6 **villainy**: unlawful or evil behaviour **display**: show
9 **strike a balance**: create a balance 12 **be inclined to do sth.**: want to do sth.
13 **accusation**: claim that sb. has done sth. wrong 16 **suffocate sb.**: stop sb. from getting enough air 21 **take vengeance**: do sth. bad to sb. who has harmed you before; take revenge **charitable**: kind to others, especially **injunction** (fml): order from someone in authority 22 **land-lust**: greed for land 22–23 **bicker over sth.**: fight about sth. unimportant 23 **boundary**: a (visible or invisible) line that separates two pieces of land **deed** (legal): written document signed by everybody involved, usually stating that you own sth. **elevate**: make more important
23 **arena** (fig.): public sphere where disagreements are debated 24 **cry witch against sb.**: accuse sb. of being a witch

perfectly justified in the bargain. Old scores could be settled on a plane of heavenly combat between Lucifer and the Lord; suspicions and the envy of the miserable toward the happy could and did burst out in the general revenge.

[REVEREND PARRIS *is praying now, and, though we cannot hear his words, a sense of his confusion hangs about him. He mumbles, then seems about to weep; then he weeps, then prays again; but his daughter does not stir on the bed.*
The door opens, and his Negro slave enters. TITUBA *is in her forties.* PARRIS *brought her with him from Barbados, where he spent some years as a merchant before entering the ministry. She enters as one does who can no longer bear to be barred from the sight of her beloved, but she is also very frightened because her slave sense has warned her that, as always, trouble in this house eventually lands on her back.*]

TITUBA [*already taking a step backward*]: My Betty be hearty soon?

PARRIS: Out of here!

TITUBA [*backing to the door*]: My Betty not goin' die …

PARRIS [*scrambling to his feet in a fury*]: Out of my sight! [*She is gone.*] Out of my – [*He is overcome with sobs. He clamps his teeth against them and closes the door and leans against it, exhausted.*] Oh, my God! God help me! [*Quaking with fear, mumbling to himself through his sobs, be goes to the bed and gently takes* BETTY'S *hand.*] Betty.

1 **be justified**: have the right to do sth. **in the bargain** (AE) ['bɑːgən]: in addition, also **settle an old score**: take revenge for sth. that happened in the past 2 **plane** (fig.): *Ebene* **combat**: fight, battle **Lucifer**: the devil **the Lord**: God or Christ 3 **miserable**: very unhappy 6 **mumble sth.**: say sth. unclearly or quietly 8 **stir**: move 9 **Negro** (derog.): term for a person of African origin, used in the U.S. until the 1960s, today it is very derogatory 11 **merchant**: person who buys and sells things in large amounts **ministry**: group of people in professions connected with religious service 12 **bar sb. from sth.**: keep sb. away from sth. **beloved** (old-fashioned): person you love very much 15 **hearty** (old-fashioned): healthy 19 **clamp your teeth**: press your teeth together with force 21 **quake** (old-fashioned): shake

Child. Dear child. Will you wake, will you open up your eyes! Betty, little one ...

[*He is bending to kneel again when his niece,* ABIGAIL WILLIAMS, *seventeen, enters – a strikingly beautiful girl, an orphan, with an endless capacity for dissembling. Now she is all worry and apprehension and propriety.*]

ABIGAIL: Uncle?

[*He looks to her.*]

Susanna Wakott's here from Doctor Griggs.

PARRIS: Oh? Let her come, let her come.

ABIGAIL [*leaning out the door to call to* SUSANNA, *who is down the hall a few steps*]: Come in, Susanna.

[SUSANNA WALCOTT, *a little younger than* ABIGAIL, *a nervous, hurried girl, enters.*]

PARRIS [*eagerly*]: What does the doctor say, child?

SUSANNA [*craning around* PARRIS *to get a look at* BETTY]: He bid me come and tell you, reverend sir, that he cannot discover no medicine for it in his books.

PARRIS: Then he must search on.

SUSANNA: Aye, sir, he have been searchin' his books since he left you, sir. But he bid me tell you, that you might look to unnatural things for the cause of it.

PARRIS [*his eyes going wide*]: No – no. There be no unnatural cause here. Tell him I have sent for Reverend Hale of Beverly, and Mr Hale will surely confirm that. Let him look to medicine and put out all thought of unnatural causes here. There be none.

SUSANNA: Aye, sir. He bid me tell you. [*She turns to go.*]

4 **orphan**: child whose mother and father have died 5 **capacity**: ability **dissemble**: act differently from how you really feel **apprehension**: fear 6 **propriety [prə'praɪəti]**: correct behaviour 16 **crane**: bend or stretch your body or neck 24 **reverend**: term used to address a clergyman 25 **confirm sth.**: say that sth. is really true

ABIGAIL: Speak nothin' of it in the village, Susanna.

PARRIS: Go directly home and speak nothing of unnatural causes.

SUSANNA: Aye, sir. I pray for her. [*She goes out.*]

ABIGAIL: Uncle, the rumour of witchcraft is all about; I think you'd best go down and deny it yourself. The parlour's packed with people, sir. I'll sit with her.

PARRIS [*pressed, turns on her*]: And what shall I say to them? That my daughter and my niece I discovered dancing like heathen in the forest?

ABIGAIL: Uncle, we did dance; let you tell them I confessed it – and I'll be whipped if I must be. But they're speakin' of witchcraft. Betty's not witched.

PARRIS: Abigail, I cannot go before the congregation when I know you have not opened with me. What did you do with her in the forest?

ABIGAIL: We did dance, uncle, and when you leaped out of the bush so suddenly, Betty was frightened and then she fainted. And there's the whole of it.

PARRIS: Child. Sit you down.

ABIGAIL [*quavering, as she sits*]: I would never hurt Betty. I love her dearly.

PARRIS: Now look you, child, your punishment will come in its time. But if you trafficked with spirits in the forest I must know it now, for surely my enemies will, and they will ruin me with it.

4 **rumour**: information passed from one person to the next which may not be true **witchcraft**: ability to do magic 5 **parlour** (old-fashioned): living-room 10 **confess sth.**: admit to have done sth. wrong 13 **congregation**: group of people who regularly come to the same church 15 **open with sb.** (old-fashioned): tell sb. the truth 23 **traffick with sb.** (old use): be in contact with sb.

ABIGAIL: But we never conjured spirits.

PARRIS: Then why can she not move herself since midnight? This child is desperate!
[ABIGAIL *lowers her eyes.*]
It must come out – my enemies will bring it out. Let me know what you done there. Abigail, do you understand that I have many enemies?

ABIGAIL: I have heard of it, uncle.

PARRIS: There is a faction that is sworn to drive me from my pulpit. Do you understand that?

ABIGAIL: I think so, sir.

PARRIS: Now then, in the midst of such disruption, my own household is discovered to be the very centre of some obscene practice. Abominations are done in the forest –

ABIGAIL: It were sport, uncle!

PARRIS [*pointing at* BETTY]: You call this sport? [*She lowers her eyes. He pleads.*] Abigail, if you know something that may help the doctor, for God's sake tell it to me. [*She is silent.*] I saw Tituba waving her arms over the fire when I came on you. Why was she doing that? And I heard a screeching and gibberish coming from her mouth. She were swaying like a dumb beast over that fire!

ABIGAIL: She always sings her Barbados songs, and we dance.

1 **conjure sth.**: make sth. appear by magic **spirit** (old-fashioned): supernatural being 3 **desperate**: in great danger 9 **faction**: group of people within a larger group with different opinions or aims than the rest **pulpit** **['pʊlpɪt]**: place in a church from which the priest addresses the congregation 12 **disruption**: (here) difficulties 13 **obscene**: *obszön* 14 **abomination**: an extremely bad and disgusting thing 15 **sport** (old-fashioned): fun 19 **come on sb.** (fml): meet sb. accidentally 20 **screech** **[skriːtʃ]**: make a high, horrible sound **gibberish** **['dʒɪbərɪʃ]**: meaningless words 21 **sway**: move slowly from side to side **dumb**: (here) stupid **beast**: wild animal

PARRIS: I cannot blink what I saw, Abigail, for my enemies will not blink it. I saw a dress lying on the grass.

ABIGAIL [*innocently*]: A dress?

PARRIS [*it is very hard to say*]: Aye, a dress. And I thought I saw – someone naked running through the trees!

ABIGAIL [*in terror*]: No one was naked! You mistake yourself, uncle!

PARRIS [*with anger*]: I saw it! [*He moves from her. Then, resolved*] Now tell me true, Abigail. And I pray you feel the weight of truth upon you, for now my ministry's at stake, my ministry and perhaps your cousin's life. Whatever abomination you have done, give me all of it now, for I dare not be taken unaware when I go before them down there.

ABIGAIL: There is nothin' more. I swear it, uncle.

PARRIS [*studies her, then nods, half convinced*]: Abigail, I have fought here three long years to bend these stiff-necked people to me, and now, just now when some good respect is rising for me in the parish, you compromise my very character. I have given you a home, child, I have put clothes upon your back – now give me upright answer. Your name in the town – it is entirely white, is it not?

ABIGAIL [*with an edge of resentment*]: Why, I am sure it, sir. There be no blush about my name.

PARRIS [*to the point*]: Abigail, is there any other cause than you have told me, for your being discharged from Goody Proctor's service? I have heard it said, and I tell you as I heard it, that she comes so

1 **blink** (old use): ignore 6 **mistake oneself** (old-fashioned): be wrong 8 **tell sb. true** (old use): tell sb. the truth 11 **be taken unaware**: be faced with sth. unexpected 15 **stiff-necked**: arrogant and traditional 17 **parish**: area that belongs to a particular church 19 **upright** (old-fashioned): (here) true **name**: (here) reputation **white**: (here) good 21 **edge**: a tone in your voice **resentment**: bad feelings about sth. you find unfair 22 **blush** (old use): shame 24 **discharge sb.**: fire sb. **Goody** (old use): polite form of address for a woman

rarely to the church this year for she will not sit so close to something soiled. What signified that remark?

ABIGAIL: She hates me, uncle, she must, for I would not be her slave. It's a bitter woman, a lying, cold, snivelling woman, and I will not work for such a woman!

PARRIS: She may be. And yet it has troubled me that you are now seven month out of their house, and in all this time no other family has ever called for your service.

ABIGAIL: They want slaves, not such as I. Let them send to Barbados for that. I will not black my face for any of them! [*With ill-concealed resentment at him*] Do you begrudge my bed, uncle?

PARRIS: No – no.

ABIGAIL [*in a temper*]: My name is good in the village! I will not have it said my name is soiled! Goody Proctor is a gossiping liar! [*Enter* MRS ANN PUTNAM. *She is a twisted soul of forty-five, a death-ridden woman, haunted by dreams.*]

PARRIS [*as soon as the door begins to open*]: No – no, I cannot have anyone. [*He sees her, and a certain deference springs into him, although his worry remains.*] Why, Goody Putnam, come in.

MRS PUTNAM [*full of breath, shiny-eyed*]: It is a marvel. It is surely a stroke of hell upon you.

PARRIS: No, Goody Putnam, it is –

MRS PUTNAM [*glancing at Betty*]: How high did she fly, how high?

PARRIS: No, no, she never flew –

2 **soiled**: dirty **signify**: mean 4 **snivelling**: (here) pathetic 10 **black** (v; old use): make dirty 10–11 **ill-concealed** (fml): badly hidden 11 **begrudge sb. sth.**: feel that sb. doesn't deserve sth. 14 **gossip**: talk about other people, often saying bad things 15 **twisted**: strange 15–16 **death-ridden**: obsessed with thoughts of death 16 **haunted**: obsessed; worried 18 **deference**: respect 19 **why** (interjection; AE): expressing surprise

MRS PUTNAM [*very pleased with it*]: Why, it's sure she did. Mr Collins saw her goin' over Ingersoll's barn, and come down light as bird, he says!

PARRIS: Now, look you, Goody Putnam, she never – [*Enter* THOMAS PUTNAM, *a well-to-do, hard-handed landowner, near fifty*.] Oh, good morning, Mr Putnam.

PUTNAM: It is a providence the thing is out now! It is a providence. [*He goes directly to the bed*.]

PARRIS: What's out, sir, what's – ?
[MRS PUTNAM *goes to the bed*.]

PUTNAM [*looking down at* BETTY]: Why, *her* eyes is closed! Look you, Ann.

MRS PUTNAM: Why, that's strange. [*To* PARRIS] Ours is open.

PARRIS [*shocked*]: Your Ruth is sick?

MRS PUTNAM [*with vicious certainty*]: I'd not call it sick; the Devil's touch is heavier than sick. It's death, y'know, it's death drivin' into them, forked and hoofed.

PARRIS: Oh, pray not! Why, how does Ruth ail?

MRS PUTNAM: She ails as she must – she never waked this morning, but her eyes open and she walks, and hears naught, sees naught, and cannot eat. Her soul is taken, surely.
[PARRIS *is struck*.]

PUTNAM [*as though for further details*]: They say you've sent for Reverend Hale of Beverly?

PARRIS [*with dwindling convinction now*]: A precaution only. He has much experience in all demonic arts, and I –

7 **providence**: holy sign 17 **forked and hoofed**: with horns and hooves; referring to the devil 18 **pray** (interjection; old use): please **ail**: be ill 19 **waked** (old use): past form of wake 20 **naught** (old use) [nɔːt]: nothing 25 **dwindle**: become smaller **precaution** [prɪˈkɔːʃn]: sth. you do to stop bad things happening
26 **demonic arts**: things done by evil spirits

MRS PUTNAM: He has indeed; and found a witch in Beverly last year, and let you remember that.

PARRIS: Now, Goody Ann, they only thought that were a witch, and I am certain there be no element of witchcraft here.

PUTNAM: No witchcraft! Now look you, Mr Parris –

PARRIS: Thomas, Thomas, I pray you, leap not to witchcraft. I know that you – you least of all, Thomas, would ever wish so disastrous a charge laid upon me. We cannot leap to witchcraft. They will howl me out of Salem for such corruption in my house.

A word about Thomas Putnam. He was a man with many grievances, at least one of which appears justified. Some time before, his wife's brother-in-law, James Bayley, had been turned down as minister of Salem. Bayley had all the qualifications, and a two-thirds vote into the bargain, but a faction stopped his acceptance, for reasons that are not clear.

Thomas Putnam was the eldest son of the richest man in the village. He had fought the Indians at Narragansett, and was deeply interested in parish affairs. He undoubtedly felt it poor payment that the village should so blatantly disregard his candidate for one of its more important offices, especially since he regarded himself as the intellectual superior of most of the people around him.

His vindictive nature was demonstrated long before the witchcraft began. Another former Salem minister, George Burroughs, had had to borrow money to pay for his wife's funeral, and, since the parish was remiss in his salary, he was soon bankrupt. Thomas and his

5 **look you** (old use): watch out! 6 **leap to sth.**: have an opinion about sth. without knowing all the facts 7 **disastrous**: very bad 8 **lay a charge upon sb.**: accuse sb. of sth. 9 **howl sb. out (of a place)**: chase sb. away 10 **grievance**: complaint 12 **brother-in-law**: the brother of a man's wife, or the husband of his sister **turn sb. down**: reject sb. **minister**: priest, preacher 17 **Narragansett**: area on Rhode Island where native Americans were defeated by English settlers in 1678 18 **poor payment** (fig.): insufficient reward 19 **blatantly** **['bleɪtəntli]**: doing sth. openly **disregard sth./sb.**: ignore sth. or sb. 21 **superior** (n): sb. who is better than others 22 **vindictive**: wanting to harm those who have offended you in the past 25 **be remiss in sth.**: (here) not having paid sth.

brother John had Burroughs jailed for debts the man did not owe. The incident is important only in that Burroughs succeeded in becoming minister where Bayley, Thomas Putnam's brother-in-law, had been rejected; the motif of resentment is clear here. Thomas Putnam felt that his own name and the honour of his family had been smirched by the village, and he meant to right matters however he could.

Another reason to believe him a deeply embittered man was his attempt to break his father's will, which left a disproportionate amount to a stepbrother. As with every other public cause in which he tried to force his way, he failed in this.

So it is not surprising to find that so many accusations against people are in the handwriting of Thomas Putnam, or that his name is so often found as a witness corroborating the supernatural testimony, or that his daughter led the crying-out at the most opportune junctures of the trials, especially when – But we'll speak of that when we come to it.

PUTNAM [*at the moment he is intent upon getting* PARRIS, *for whom he has only contempt, to move toward the abyss*]: Mr Parris, I have taken your part in all contention here, and I would continue; but I cannot if you hold back in this. There are hurtful, vengeful spirits layin' hands on these children.

PARRIS: But, Thomas, you cannot –

1 **jail sb.** (v): put sb. in prison 4 **motif** (old spelling): theme 6 **smirch sth.**: make sth. dirty **right** (v): put right; correct 8 **embittered**: angry or sad because bad things happened to you 9 **break sb.'s will**: *ein Testament aufheben* **disproportionate** [ˌdɪsprəˈpɔːʃənət]: (here) very large 10 **cause**: (here) a legal action 14 **witness** (n): sb. who has seen sth. happen **corrobrate**: proove a statement or idea **testimony**: official statement (e.g. in court) 15–16 **opportune juncture** (fml): the right moment 18 **be intent upon doing sth.**: put a lot of effort into doing sth. 19 **abyss**: seemingly bottomless hole in the ground 20 **contention**: strong disagreement among two people 21 **hurtful**: wanting to hurt people **vengeful**: wanting to hurt sb. for having hurt you

PUTNAM: Ann! Tell Mr Parris what you have done.

MRS PUTNAM: Reverend Parris, I have laid seven babies unbaptized in the earth. Believe me, sir, you never saw more hearty babies born. And yet, each would wither in my arms the very night of their birth. I have spoke nothin', but my heart has clamoured intimations. And now, this year, my Ruth, my only – I see her turning strange. A secret child she has become this year, and shrivels like a sucking mouth were puffin' on her life too. And so I thought to send her to your Tituba –

PARRIS: To Tituba! What may Tituba – ?

MRS PUTNAM: Tituba knows how to speak to the dead, Mr Parris.

PARRIS: Goody Ann, it is a formidable sin to conjure up the dead!

MRS PUTNAM: I take it on my soul, but who else may surely tell us what person murdered my babies?

PARRIS [*horrified*]: Woman!

MRS PUTNAM: They were murdered, Mr Parris! And mark this proof! Mark it! Last night my Ruth were ever so close to their little spirits; I know it, sir. For how else is she struck dumb now except some power of darkness would stop her mouth? It is a marvellous sign, Mr Parris!

PUTNAM: Don't you understand it, sir? There is a murdering witch among us, bound to keep herself in the dark. [PARRIS *turns to* BETTY, *a frantic terror rising in him.*] Let your enemies make of it what they will, you cannot blink it more.

2 **unbaptized**: *nicht getauft* 4 **wither**: become weaker 5 **clamour sth.** (old use) **['klæmə(r)]**: demand very loudly 6 **intimation**: hint, indirect sign 7 **secret**: (here) secretive; hiding your thoughts or feelings from others 8 **shrivel**: get smaller and wrinkled because of old age or illness 12 **formidable**: very big and terrible 15 **horrified**: extremely scared or shocked 17 **mark sth.**: (here) pay attention to sth. 18 **struck dumb**: suddenly unable to speak 20 **marvellous** (old-fashioned): (here) amazing 22 **be bound to do sth.**: be forced to do sth. 23 **frantic**: uncontrollable

PARRIS [*to* ABIGAIL]: Then you were conjuring spirits last night.

ABIGAIL [*whispering*]: Not I, sir – Tituba and Ruth.

PARRIS [*turns now, with new fear, and goes to* BETTY, *looks down at her, and then, gazing off*]: Oh, Abigail, what proper payment for my charity! Now I am undone.

PUTNAM: You are not undone! Let you take hold here. Wait for no one to charge you – declare it yourself. You have discovered witchcraft –

PARRIS: In my house? In my house, Thomas? They will topple me with this! They will make of it a –
[*Enter* MERCY LEWIS, *the Putnams' servant, a fat, sly, merciless girl of eighteen.*]

MERCY: Your pardons. I only thought to see how Betty is.

PUTNAM: Why aren't you home? Who's with Ruth?

MERCY: Her grandma come. She's improved a little, I think she give a powerful sneeze before.

MRS PUTNAM: Ah, there's a sign of life!

MERCY: I'd fear no more, Goody Putnam. It were a grand sneeze; another like it will shake her wits together, I'm sure.
[*She goes to the bed to look.*]

PARRIS: Will you leave me now, Thomas? I would pray a while alone.

ABIGAIL: Uncle, you've prayed since midnight. Why do you not go down and –

5 **be undone** (old use): ruined 6 **take hold**: here: take control 7 **charge sb.**: accuse sb. of a crime 9 **topple sb.**: (here) remove sb. from a position of power 11 **sly**: dishonest **merciless**: unwilling to show pity or to forgive 16 **sneeze**: *Niesen* 19 **wits**: the mind (shake your wits together: get your mind to function properly)

PARRIS: No – no. [*To* PUTNAM] I have no answer for that crowd. I'll wait till Mr Hale arrives. [*To get* MRS PUTNAM *to leave*] If you will, Goody Ann …

PUTNAM: Now look you, sir. Let you strike out against the Devil, and the village will bless you for it! Come down, speak to them – pray with them. They're thirsting for your word, Mister! Surely you'll pray with them.

PARRIS [*swayed*]: I'll lead them in a psalm, but let you say nothing of witchcraft yet. I will not discuss it. The cause is yet unknown. I have had enough contention since I came; I want no more.

MRS PUTNAM: Mercy, you go home to Ruth, d'y'hear?

MERCY: Aye, mum.
[MRS PUTNAM *goes out.*]

PARRIS [*to* ABIGAIL]: If she starts for the window, cry for me at once.

ABIGAIL: I will, uncle.

PARRIS [to PUTNAM]: There is a terrible power in her arms today.
[*He goes out with* PUTNAM.]

ABIGAIL [*with hushed trepidation*]: How is Ruth sick?

MERCY: It's weirdish, I know not – she seems to walk like a dead one since last night.

ABIGAIL [*turns at once and goes to* BETTY, *and now, with fear in her voice*]: Betty? [BETTY *doesn't move. She shakes her.*] Now stop this! Betty! Sit up now!
[BETTY *doesn't stir.* MERCY *comes over.*]

MERCY: Have you tried beatin' her? I gave Ruth a good one and it waked her for a minute. Here, let me have her.

6 **thirst for sth.**: want sth. very much 8 **swayed**: made to change your mind
12 **mum**: Madam 18 **hushed**: quiet **trepidation**: fear 19 **weirdish** ['wɪədɪʃ]: strange 25 **give sb. a good one** (infml): beat sb.

ABIGAIL [*holding* MERCY *back*]: No, he'll be comin' up. Listen, now; if they be questioning us, tell them we danced – I told him as much already.

MERCY: Aye. And what more?

ABIGAIL: He knows Tituba conjured Ruth's sisters to come out of the grave.

MERCY: And what more?

ABIGAIL: He saw you naked.

MERCY [*clapping her hands together with a frightened laugh*]: Oh, Jesus! [*Enter* MARY WARREN, *breathless. She is seventeen, a subservient, naïve, lonely girl.*]

MARY WARREN: What'll we do? The village is out! I just come from the farm; the whole country's talkin' witchcraft! They'll be callin' us witches, Abby!

MERCY [*pointing and looking at* MARY WARREN]: She means to tell, I know it.

MARY WARREN: Abby, we've got to tell. Witchery's a hangin' error, a hangin' like they done in Boston two year ago! We must tell the truth, Abby! You'll only be whipped for dancin', and the other things!

ABIGAIL: Oh, we'll be whipped!

MARY WARREN: I never done none of it, Abby. I only looked!

MERCY [*moving menacingly toward* MARY]: Oh, you're a great one for lookin', aren't you, Mary Warren? What a grand peeping courage you have!
[BETTY, *on the bed, whimpers.* ABIGAIL *turns to her at once.*]

10 **subservient**: trying to please sb. by obeying them 12 **the village is out**: all the villagers are talking in the streets 17 **hanging error**: crime for which one gets hanged 21 **whip sb.**: *jdn. auspeitschen* 23 **menacingly**: in a manner that makes others expect sth. bad to happen 24 **peep**: look secretly at sth. one is not supposed to see 26 **whimper**: make a noise as if crying

ABIGAIL: Betty? [*She goes to* BETTY.] Now, Betty, dear, wake up now. It's Abigail. [*She sits* BETTY *up and furiously shakes her.*] I'll beat you, Betty! [BETTY *whimpers.*] My, you seem improving. I talked to your papa and I told him everything. So there's nothing to –

BETTY [*darts off the bed, frightened of* ABIGAIL, *and flattens herself against the wall*]: I want my mama!

ABIGAIL [*with alarm, as she cautiously approaches* BETTY]: What ails you, Betty? Your mama's dead and buried.

BETTY: I'll fly to Mama. Let me fly! [*She raises her arms as though to fly, and streaks for the window, gets one leg out.*]

ABIGAIL [*pulling her away from the window*]: I told him everything; he knows now, he knows everything we –

BETTY: You drank blood, Abby! You didn't tell him that!

ABIGAIL: Betty, you never say that again! You will never –

BETTY: You did, you did! You drank a charm to kill John Proctor's wife! You drank a charm to kill Goody Proctor!

ABIGAIL [*smashes her across the face*]: Shut it! Now shut it!

BETTY [*collapsing on the bed*]: Mama, Mama! [*She dissolves into sobs.*]

ABIGAIL: Now look you. All of you. We danced. And Tituba conjured Ruth Putnam's dead sisters. And that is all. And mark this. Let either of you breathe a word, or the edge of a word, about the other things, and I will come to you in the black of some terrible night and I will bring a pointy reckoning that will shudder you. And you know I can do it; I saw Indians smash my dear parents' heads on the pillow next to mine, and I have seen some reddish

2 **furiously**: in a very angry way 3 **my** (interjection): now; well 5 **dart**: move quickly and suddenly 5–6 **flatten oneself against sth.**: press one's body against sth. 7 **alarm**: (here) fear 10 **streak**: move extremely fast 15 **charm**: sth. that has supernatural or magical effects 17 **smash sb.**: (here) hit sb. 21 **breathe a word about sth.**: mention sth. **edge**: (here) slight hint 23 **pointy**: sharp (e.g. intended to hurt) **reckoning**: punishment **shudder sb.**: scare sb. so much that they shake

work done at night, and I can make you wish you had never seen the sun go down! [*She goes to* BETTY *and roughly sits her up.*] Now, you – sit up and stop this!

[*But* BETTY *collapses in her hands and lies inert on the bed.*]

MARY WARREN [*with hysterical fright*]: What's got her? [ABIGAIL *stares in fright at* BETTY.] Abby, she's going to die! It's a sin to conjure, and we –

ABIGAIL [*starting for* MARY]: I say shut it, Mary Warren!

[*Enter* JOHN PROCTOR. *On seeing him,* MARY WARREN *leaps in fright.*]

Proctor was a farmer in his middle thirties. He need not have been a partisan of any faction in the town, but there is evidence to suggest that he had a sharp and biting way with hypocrites. He was the kind of man – powerful of body, even-tempered, and not easily led – who cannot refuse support to partisans without drawing their deepest resentment. In Proctor's presence a fool felt his foolishness instantly – and a Proctor is always marked for calumny therefore.

But as we shall see, the steady manner he displays does not spring from an untroubled soul. He is a sinner, a sinner not only against the moral fashion of the time, but against his own vision of decent conduct. These people had no ritual for the washing away of sins. It is another trait we inherited from them, and it has helped to discipline us as well as to breed hypocrisy among us. Proctor, respected and even feared in Salem, has come to regard himself as a kind of fraud. But no hint of this has yet appeared on the surface, and as he enters from the crowded parlour below it is a man in his

5 **fright**: fear 12 **partisan**: strong supporter of a particular group or idea 13 **hypocrite ['hɪpəkrɪt]**: person who pretends to follow moral standards which they secretly break 14 **even-tempered**: calm 15 **draw**: (here) attract 15 **be marked for**: be chosen for **calumny**: negative things said about a person in order to make others think badly about them 20 **decent**: morally good 21 **conduct**: behaviour 22 **trait**: particular quality in your personality **inherit**: get sth. from a person after they die 23 **hypocrisy**: behaviour of a hypocrite 25 **fraud**: person who pretends to be sth. that they are not

prime we see, with a quiet confidence and an unexpressed, hidden force. Mary Warren, his servant, can barely speak for embarrassment and fear.

MARY WARREN: Oh! I'm just going home, Mr Proctor.

PROCTOR: Be you foolish, Mary Warren? Be you deaf? I forbid you leave the house, did I not? Why shall I pay you? I am looking for you more often than my cows!

MARY WARREN: I only come to see the great doings in the world.

PROCTOR: I'll show you a great doin' on your arse one of these days. Now get you home; my wife is waitin' with your work!
[*Trying to retain a shred of dignity, she goes slowly out.*]

MERCY LEWIS [*both afraid of him and strangely titillated*]: I'd best be off. I have my Ruth to watch. Good morning, Mr Proctor.
[MERCY *sidles out. Since* PROCTOR'S *entrance,* ABIGAIL *has stood as though on tiptoe, absorbing his presence, wide-eyed. He glances at her, then goes to* BETTY *on the bed.*]

ABIGAIL: Gah! I'd almost forgot how strong you are, John Proctor!

PROCTOR [*looking at* ABIGAIL *now, the faintest suggestion of a knowing smile on his face*]: What's this mischief here?

ABIGAIL [*with a nervous laugh*]: Oh, she's only gone silly somehow.

PROCTOR: The road past my house is a pilgrimage to Salem all morning. The town's mumbling witchcraft.

2 **embarrassment**: uncomfortable feeling 9 **arse** (derog.): *Arsch* 11 **shred of sth.**: small piece of sth. **dignity**: *Würde* 12 **titillated**: excited (often sexually) 14 **sidle**: walk quietly so that you are not noticed 15 **absorb sth.**: take sth. in 17 **Gah!** (interjection): God! 18 **faint**: (here) subtle **suggestion**: hint 19 **mischief** (fml) ['mɪstʃɪf]: problem 21 **pilgrimage** ['pɪlgrɪmɪdʒ]: journey to a religious place; (here) implying that lots of people are walking around for a special purpose

ABIGAIL: Oh, posh! [*Winningly she comes a little closer, with a confidential, wicked air.*] We were dancin' in the woods last night, and my uncle leaped in on us. She took fright, is all.

PROCTOR [*his smile widening*]: Ah, you're wicked yet, aren't y'! [*A trill of expectant laughter escapes her, and she dares come closer, feverishly looking into his eyes.*]
You'll be clapped in the stocks before you're twenty.
[*He takes a step to go, and she springs into his path.*]

ABIGAIL: Give me a word, John. A soft word. [*Her concentrated desire destroys his smile.*]

PROCTOR: No, no, Abby. That's done with.

ABIGAIL [*tauntingly*]: You come five mile to see a silly girl fly? I know you better.

PROCTOR [*setting her firmly out of his path*]: I come to see what mischief your uncle's brewin' now. [*With final emphasis*] Put it out of mind, Abby.

ABIGAIL [*grasping his hand before he can release her*]: John – I am waitin' for you every night.

PROCTOR: Abby, I never give you hope to wait for me.

ABIGAIL [*now beginning to anger – she can't believe it*]: I have something better than hope, I think!

PROCTOR: Abby, you'll put it out of mind. I'll not be comin' for you more.

ABIGAIL: You're surely sportin' with me.

1 **posh!**: (here) nonsense! 1–2 **confidential**: (here) showing that you know sb. well 2 **wicked ['wɪkɪd]**: (here) naughty 5 **trill**: high sound **expectant**: expressing that you are hoping for sth. 7 **be clapped in the stocks**: *an den Pranger gestellt werden* 9 **soft**: (here) loving 11 **be done with**: be finished 12 **tauntingly ['tɔːntɪŋli]**: trying to make sb. angry 15 **brew sth. [bruː]**: (here) come up with sth. **emphasis**: stressing that what you say is very important 20 **anger** (v): (here) get angry 24 **sport with sb.**: play games with sb.

PROCTOR: You know me better.

ABIGAIL: I know how you clutched my back behind your house and sweated like a stallion whenever I come near! Or did I dream that? It's she put me out, you cannot pretend it were you. I saw your face when she put me out, and you loved me then and you do now!

PROCTOR: Abby, that's a wild thing to say –

ABIGAIL: A wild thing may say wild things. But not so wild, I think. I have seen you since she put me out; I have seen you nights.

PROCTOR: I have hardly stepped off my farm this seven-month.

ABIGAIL: I have a sense for heat, John, and yours has drawn me to my window, and I have seen you looking up, burning in your loneliness. Do you tell me you've never looked up at my window?

PROCTOR: I may have looked up.

ABIGAIL [*now softening*]: And you must. You are no wintry man. I know you, John. I know you. [*She is weeping.*] I cannot sleep for dreamin'; I cannot dream but I wake and walk about the house as though I'd find you comin' through some door. [*She clutches him desperately.*]

PROCTOR [*gently pressing her from him, with great sympathy but firmly*]: Child –

ABIGAIL [*with a flash of anger*]: How do you call me child!

PROCTOR: Abby, I may think of you softly from time to time. But I will cut off my hand before I'll ever reach for you again. Wipe it out of mind. We never touched, Abby.

ABIGAIL: Aye, but we did.

PROCTOR: Aye, but we did not.

2 **clutch sth.**: hold on to sth. very firmly 3 **stallion**: male horse 4 **put sb. out**: send sb. away 15 **wintry**: cold 20 **sympathy**: understanding people's problems and feeling sorry for them

ABIGAIL [*with a bitter anger*]: Oh, I marvel how such a strong man may let such a sickly wife be –

PROCTOR [*angered – at himself as well*]: You'll speak nothin' of Elizabeth!

ABIGAIL: She is blackening my name in the village! She is telling lies about me! She is a cold, snivelling woman, and you bend to her! Let her turn you like a –

PROCTOR [*shaking her*]: Do you look for whippin'?
[*A psalm is heard being sung below.*]

ABIGAIL [*in tears*]: I look for John Proctor that took me from my sleep and put knowledge in my heart! I never knew what pretence Salem was, I never knew the lying lessons I was taught by all these Christian women and their covenanted men! And now you bid me tear the light out of my eyes? I will not, I cannot! You loved me, John Proctor, and whatever sin it is, you love me yet!
[*He turns abruptly to go out. She rushes to him.*]
John, pity me, pity me!
[*The words 'going up to Jesus' are heard in the psalm, and* BETTY *claps her ears suddenly and whines loudly.*]

ABIGAIL: Betty? [*She hurries to* BETTY, *who is now sitting up and screaming.* PROCTOR *goes to* BETTY *as* ABIGAIL *is trying to pull her hands down, calling 'Betty!'*]

PROCTOR [*growing unnerved*]: What's she doing? Girl, what ails you? Stop that wailing!
[*The singing has stopped in the midst of this, and now* PARRIS *rushes in.*]

PARRIS: What happened? What are you doing to her? Betty! [*He rushes to the bed, crying, 'Betty, Betty!'* MRS PUTNAM *enters, feverish*

1 **marvel** (v): express wonder or strong surprise 5 **blacken sb.'s name**: talk badly about sb. so that other people lose respect for that person 11 **pretence**: hypocrisy 13 **covenanted**: (here) married 19 **whine**: high-pitched wail (e.g. to complain) 23 **unnerved**: nervous

with curiosity, and with her THOMAS PUTNAM *and* MERCY LEWIS. PARRIS, *at the bed, keeps lightly slapping* BETTY'S *face, while she moans and tries to get up.*]

ABIGAIL: She heard you singin' and suddenly she's up and screamin'.

MRS PUTNAM: The psalm! The psalm! She cannot bear to hear the Lord's name!

PARRIS: No, God forbid. Mercy, run to the doctor! Tell him what's happened here! [MERCY LEWIS *rushes out.*]

MRS PUTNAM: Mark it for a sign, mark it!

[REBECCA NURSE, *seventy-two, enters. She is white-haired, leaning upon her walking-stick.*]

PUTNAM [*pointing at the whimpering* BETTY]: That is a notorious sign of witchcraft afoot, Goody Nurse, a prodigious sign!

MRS PUTNAM: My mother told me that! When they cannot bear to hear the name of –

PARRIS [*trembling*]: Rebecca, Rebecca, go to her, we're lost. She suddenly cannot bear to hear the Lord's –

[GILES COREY, *eighty-three, enters. He is knotted with muscle, canny, inquisitive, and still powerful.*]

REBECCA: There is hard sickness here, Giles Corey, so please to keep the quiet.

GILES: I've not said a word. No one here can testify I've said a word. Is she going to fly again? I hear she flies.

PUTNAM: Man, be quiet now!

2 **slap sth.**: hit sth. with the palm of your hand 3 **moan**: make a long, low sound
7 **God forbid** (interjection): expressing that you hope sth. won't happen
12 **notorious**: well-known in a negative way 13 **be afoot**: be happening
prodigious (old use) **[prəˈdɪdʒəs]**: a sign of sth. bad about to happen 18 **knotted with muscle** [ˈnɒtɪd]: with lots of muscles **canny**: clever 19 **inquisitive** [ɪnˈkwɪzətɪv]: wanting to find out more about things 22 **testify**: say that sth. is true

[*Everything is quiet.* REBECCA *walks across the room to the bed. Gentleness exudes from her.* BETTY *is quietly whimpering, eyes shut.* REBECCA *simply stands over the child, who gradually quiets.*]

And while they are so absorbed, we may put a word in for Rebecca. Rebecca was the wife of Francis Nurse, who, from all accounts, was one of those men for whom both sides of the argument had to have respect. He was called upon to arbitrate disputes as though he were an unofficial judge, and Rebecca also enjoyed the high opinion most people had for him. By the time of the delusion, they had three hundred acres, and their children were settled in separate homesteads within the same estate. However, Francis had originally rented the land, and one theory has it that, as he gradually paid for it and raised his social status, there were those who resented his rise.

Another suggestion to explain the systematic campaign against Rebecca, and inferentially against Francis, is the land war he fought with his neighbours, one of whom was a Putnam. This squabble grew to the proportions of a battle in the woods between partisans of both sides, and it is said to have lasted for two days. As for Rebecca herself, the general opinion of her character was so high that to explain how anyone dared cry her out for a witch – and more, how adults could bring themselves to lay hands on her – we must look to the fields and boundaries of that time.

As we have seen, Thomas Putnam's man for the Salem ministry was Bayley. The Nurse clan had been in the faction that prevented Bayley's taking office. In addition, certain families allied to the Nurses by blood or friendship, and whose farms were contiguous with the Nurse farm or close to it, combined to break away from the

2 **exude**: clearly show a quality that you have 4 **be absorbed**: pay attention to one thing and nothing else 5 **account**: description 7 **arbitrate**: help find a solution to an argument **dispute**: argument 9 **delusion** [dɪ'luːʒn]: false idea that sth. is true 10 **acre**: an area of land (4047 square metres) **homestead** ['həʊmsted]: house with farmland around it 11 **estate**: alarge piece of land owned by one family 13 **resent sth.**: feel angry about sth. 15 **inferentially**: as a consequence 16 **squabble**: argument about unimportant things 20 **cry sb. out for sth.**: accuse sb. of being sth. 24 **clan**: large family 25 **allied to**: connected with 26 **be contiguous with sth.** [kən'tɪgjuəs]: be very close to sth.

Salem town authority and set up Topsfield, a new and independent entity whose existence was resented by old Salemites.

That the guiding hand behind the outcry was Putnam's is indicated by the fact that, as soon as it began, this Topsfield-Nurse faction absented themselves from church in protest and disbelief. It was Edward and Jonathan Putnam who signed the first complaint against Rebecca; and Thomas Putnam's little daughter was the one who fell into a fit at the hearing and pointed to Rebecca as her attacker. To top it all, Mrs Putnam – who is now staring at the bewitched child on the bed – soon accused Rebecca's spirit of 'tempting her to iniquity', a charge that had more truth in it than Mrs Putnam could know.

MRS PUTNAM [*astonished*]: What have you done?

[REBECCA, *in thought, now leaves the bedside and sits.*]

PARRIS [*wondrous and relieved*]: What do you make of it, Rebecca?

PUTNAM [*eagerly*]: Goody Nurse, will you go to my Ruth and see if you can wake her?

REBECCA [*sitting*]: I think she'll wake in time. Pray calm yourselves. I have eleven children, and I am twenty-six times a grandma, and I have seen them all through their silly seasons, and when it come on them they will run the Devil bowlegged keeping up with their mischief. I think she'll wake when she tires of it. A child's spirit is like a child, you can never catch it by running after it; you must stand still, and, for love, it will soon itself come back.

1 **town authority**: town government 2 **entity**: unit **Salemite**: sb. who lives in Salem 3 **outcry**: loud protest 5 **absent oneself from sth.**: stay away from sth. **disbelief**: not believing 6 **complaint**: (here) piece of writing stating that sth. is wrong 8 **fall into a fit**: suffer a sudden attack of an illness (e.g. epilepsy) **hearing** (n): a meeting at which a crime or accusation is examined 9 **to top it all**: term introducing information that is stronger or worse than everything mentioned before 11 **tempt sb. to sth.**: encourage sb. to do sth. **iniquity**: state of being very bad or unfair 15 **wondrous** (old-fashioned): amazed 15 **What do you make of it?**: What do you think about this? 20 **season**: (here) phase 20–21 **when it come on them**: when they are in that phase 21 **bowlegged**: with crooked legs

PROCTOR: Aye, that's the truth of it, Rebecca.

MRS PUTNAM: This is no silly season, Rebecca. My Ruth is bewildered, Rebecca; she cannot eat.

REBECCA: Perhaps she is not hungered yet. [*To* PARRIS] I hope you are not decided to go in search of loose spirits, Mr Parris. I've heard promise of that outside.

PARRIS: A wide opinion's running in the parish that the Devil may be among us, and I would satisfy them that they are wrong.

PROCTOR: Then let you come out and call them wrong. Did you consult the wardens before you called this minister to look for devils?

PARRIS: He is not coming to look for devils

PROCTOR: Then what's he coming for?

PUTNAM: There be children dyin' in the village, Mister!

PROCTOR: I seen none dyin'. This society will not be a bag to swing around your head, Mr Putnam. [*To* PARRIS] Did you call a meeting before you – ?

PUTNAM: I am sick of meetings; cannot the man turn his head without he have a meeting?

PROCTOR: He may turn his head, but not to Hell!

REBECCA: Pray, John, be calm. [*Pause. He defers to her.*] Mr Parris, I think you'd best send Reverend Hale back as soon as he come. This will set us all to arguin' again in the society, and we thought to have peace this year. I think we ought rely on the doctor now, and good prayer.

3 **bewildered**: confused 4 **hungered** (old-fashioned): hungry 5 **loose spirit**: evil spirit 6 **promise**: (here) rumour 7 **opinion**: (here) rumour 10 **warden**: person in charge (of a church) 15–16 **This society will not be a bag to swing around your head**: you cannot control this society however you want 19 **without he have** (old use): without having 21 **defer to sb.**: do as sb. wishes

MRS PUTNAM: Rebecca, the doctor's baffled!

REBECCA: If so he is, then let us go to God for the cause of it. There is prodigious danger in the seeking of loose spirits. I fear it, I fear it. Let us rather blame ourselves and –

PUTNAM: How may we blame ourselves? I am one of nine sons; the Putnam seed have peopled this province. And yet I have but one child left of eight – and now she shrivels!

REBECCA: I cannot fathom that.

MRS PUTNAM [*with a growing edge of sarcasm*]: But I must! You think it God's work you should never lose a child, nor grandchild either, and I bury all but one? There are wheels within wheels in this village, and fires within fires!

PUTNAM [*to* PARRIS]: When Reverend Hale comes, you will proceed to look for signs of witchcraft here.

PROCTOR [*to* PUTNAM]: You cannot command Mr Parris. We vote by name in this society, not by acreage.

PUTNAM: I never heard you worried so on this society, Mr Proctor. I do not think I saw you at Sabbath meeting since snow flew.

PROCTOR: I have trouble enough without I come five mile to hear him preach only hellfire and bloody damnation. Take it to heart, Mr Parris. There are many others who stay away from church these days because you hardly ever mention God any more.

PARRIS [*now aroused*]: Why, that's a drastic charge!

1 **baffled**: very confused 3 **prodigious**: very large, great 6 **people sth.** (v): fill sth. with people 8 **fathom**: understand 11 **but one** (old-fashioned): only one 11–12 **wheels within wheels, fires within fires**: term used to say that sth. is very hard to understand 13–14 **proceed to do sth.**: start to do sth. 16 **acreage**: amount of land 18 **Sabbath meeting**: Sunday service in the meeting house 20 **preach hellfire and bloody damnation**: deliver a sermon which focuses on the terrible punishments for sinners 23 **drastic**: very serious

REBECCA: It's somewhat true; there are many that quail to bring their children –

PARRIS: I do not preach for children, Rebecca. It is not the children who are unmindful of their obligations toward this ministry.

REBECCA: Are there really those unmindful?

PARRIS: I should say the better half of Salem village –

PUTNAM: And more than that!

PARRIS: Where is my wood? My contract provides I be supplied with all my firewood. I am waiting since November for a stick, and even in November I had to show my frostbitten hands like some London beggar!

GILES: You are allowed six pound a year to buy your wood, Mr Parris.

PARRIS: I regard that six pound as part of my salary. I am paid little enough without I spend six pound on firewood.

PROCTOR: Sixty, plus six for firewood –

PARRIS: The salary is sixty-six pound, Mr Proctor! I am not some preaching farmer with a book under my arm; I am a graduate of Harvard College.

GILES: Aye, and well instructed in arithmetic!

PARRIS: Mr Corey, you will look far for a man of my kind at sixty pound a year! I am not used to this poverty; I left a thrifty business in the Barbados to serve the Lord. I do not fathom it, why am I persecuted here? I cannot offer one proposition but there be a howling riot of argument. I have often wondered if the Devil be in it somewhere; I cannot understand you people otherwise.

1–2 **quail to do sth.**: be afraid to do sth.   4 **be unmindful of your obligations**: not do your duty   8 **provide sth.**: (here) say that sth. must happen
10 **frostbitten**: hurt by extreme cold   18 **graduate** (n): sb. who has finished his studies at a college or university   20 **arithmetic**: basic mathematics   22 **thrifty**: (here) economically successful   24 **proposition**: suggestion

PROCTOR: Mr Parris, you are the first minister ever did demand the deed to this house –

PARRIS: Man! Don't a minister deserve a house to live in?

PROCTOR: To live in, yes. But to ask ownership is like you shall own the meeting house itself; the last meeting I were at you spoke so long on deeds and mortgages I thought it were an auction.

PARRIS: I want a mark of confidence, is all! I am your third preacher in seven years. I do not wish to be put out like the cat whenever some majority feels the whim. You people seem not to comprehend that a minister is the Lord's man in the parish; a minister is not to be so lightly crossed and contradicted –

PUTNAM: Aye!

PARRIS: There is either obedience or the church will burn like Hell is burning!

PROCTOR: Can you speak one minute without we land in Hell again? I am sick of Hell!

PARRIS: It is not for you to say what is good for you to hear!

PROCTOR: I may speak my heart, I think!

PARRIS [*in a fury*]: What, are we Quakers? We are not Quakers here yet, Mr Proctor. And you may tell that to your followers!

PROCTOR: My followers!

PARRIS [*now he's out with it*]: There is a party in this church. I am not blind; there is a faction and a party.

1 **the first minister ever did demand**: the first minister who ever demanded
4 **ownership**: the right to own sth. 6 **mortgage** ['mɔːgɪdʒ]: money lent to sb. to buy a house 7 **mark** (n): sign 9 **feel the whim**: have a sudden idea or desire
9–10 **comprehend**: understand 11 **be crossed**: be made angry 13 **obedience**: doing what you are told 18 **speak your heart**: say what you really think
19 **Quakers**: a religious group that was persecuted by the Puritans in New England
22 **party**: group of people with an opinion that opposes that of a larger group

PROCTOR: Against you?

PUTNAM: Against him and all authority!

PROCTOR: Why, then I must find it and join it. [*There is shock among the others.*]

REBECCA: He does not mean that.

PUTNAM: He confessed it now!

PROCTOR: I mean it solemnly, Rebecca; I like not the smell of this 'authority'.

REBECCA: No, you cannot break charity with your minister. You are another kind, John. Clasp his hand, make your peace.

PROCTOR: I have a crop to sow and lumber to drag home. [*He goes angrily to the door and turns to* COREY *with a smile.*] What say you, Giles, let's find the party. He says there's a Party.

GILES: I've changed my opinion of this man, John. Mr Parris, I beg your pardon. I never thought you had so much iron in you.

PARRIS [*surprised*]: Why, thank you, Giles!

GILES: It suggests to the mind what the trouble be among us all these years. [*To all.*] Think on it. Wherefore is everybody suing everybody else? Think on it now, it's a deep thing, and dark as a pit. I have been six time in court this year –

PROCTOR [*familiarly, with warmth, although he knows he is approaching the edge of* GILES' *tolerance with this*]: Is it the Devil's fault that a man cannot say you good morning without you clap him for defamation? You're old, Giles, and you're not hearin' so well as you did.

7 **solemnly**: in a serious manner 9 **break charity with sb.** (old-fashioned): declare that you don't like sb. 11 **crop**: plants grown on a field **lumber**: trees that have been cut down for wood **drag sth.**: pull sth. 15 **iron**: (here) inner strength 18 **think on sth.**: think about sth. **sue sb.** [suː]: *jdn. anklagen* 23–24 **clap sb. for sth.** (old use): sue sb. for sth. 24 **defamation**: publicly say sth. bad about sb.

GILES [*he cannot be crossed*]: John Proctor, I have only last month collected four pound damages for you publicly sayin' I burned the roof off your house, and I –

PROCTOR [*laughing*]: I never said no such thing, but I've paid you for it, so I hope I can call you deaf without charge. Now come along, Giles, and help me drag my lumber home.

PUTNAM: A moment, Mr Proctor. What lumber is that you're draggin', if I may ask you?

PROCTOR: My lumber. From out my forest by the riverside.

PUTNAM: Why, we are surely gone wild this year. What anarchy is this? That tract is in my bounds, it's in my bounds, Mr Proctor.

PROCTOR: In your bounds! [*Indicating* REBECCA.] I bought that tract from Goody Nurse's husband five months ago.

PUTNAM: He had no right to sell it. It stands clear in my grandfather's will that all the land between the river and –

PROCTOR: Your grandfather had a habit of willing land that never belonged to him, if I may say it plain.

GILES: That's God's truth; he nearly willed away my north pasture but he knew I'd break his fingers before he'd set his name to it. Let's get your lumber home, John. I feel a sudden will to work coming on.

PUTNAM: You load one oak of mine and you'll fight to drag it home!

GILES: Aye, and we'll win too, Putnam – this fool and I. Come on! [*He turns to* PROCTOR *and starts out.*]

PUTNAM: I'll have my men on you, Corey! I'll clap a writ on you!

2 **damages**: (here) money paid to sb. that you have harmed 5 **deaf**: unable to hear 10 **go wild**: go crazy **anarchy**: (here) chaotic situation in which there is no order 11 **tract**: piece of land **bounds**: (here) the boundaries of your land 16 **will sth.** (v): leave sth. to another person after you die 18 **pasture**: piece of land with grass on which animals are kept 25 **writ [rɪt]**: legal document, telling or forbidding sb. to do sth.

[*Enter* REVEREND JOHN HALE *of Beverly*.]

Mr Hale is nearing forty, a tight-skinned, eager-eyed intellectual. This is a beloved errand for him; on being called here to ascertain witchcraft he felt the pride of the specialist whose unique knowledge has at last been publicly called for. Like almost all men of learning, he spent a good deal of his time pondering the invisible world, especially since he had himself encountered a witch in his parish not long before. That woman, however, turned into a mere pest under his searching scrutiny, and the child she had allegedly been afflicting recovered her normal behaviour after Hale had given her his kindness and a few days of rest in his own house. However, that experience never raised a doubt in his mind as to the reality of the underworld or the existence of Lucifer's many-faced lieutenants. And his belief is not to his discredit. Better minds than Hale's were – and still are – convinced that there is a society of spirits beyond our ken. One cannot help noting that one of his lines has never yet raised a laugh in any audience that has seen this play; it is his assurance that 'We cannot look to superstition in this. The Devil is precise.' Evidently we are not quite certain even now whether diabolism is holy and not to be scoffed at. And it is no accident that we should be so bemused.

Like Reverend Hale and the others on this stage, we conceive the Devil as a necessary part of a respectable view of cosmology. Ours is

1 **tight-skinned**: without wrinkles (ie. young-looking) 2 **errand**: task **ascertain sth.**: find out if sth. is true 4 **unique**: *einzigartig* 6 **ponder sth.**: think about sth. 7 **encounter**: meet 8 **a mere ...**: only a ... **pest**: (here) annoying person 9 **scrutiny**: close examination **allegedly [ə'ledʒɪdli]**: *angeblich* **afflict sb.**: make sb. suffer 12 **as to**: concerning 13 **many-faced**: occurring in many different forms **lieutenant [lef'tenənt]**: sb. who works for and helps sb. with a higher position 14 **be to sb.'s discredit**: damage sb. reputation 15–16 **beyond our ken** (old-fashioned): unknown or not understood 16 **one cannot help doing sth.**: one has to do sth. 18 **assurance**: certainty **superstition**: irrational belief in supernatural causes or the existence of good and bad luck 19 **evidently**: clearly 20 **diabolism**: devil-worship **scoff at sth.**: make fun of sth. 21 **bemused**: confused 22–23 **conceive sth. as sth.**: understand sth. to be sth. 23 **view of cosmology**: world view

a divided empire in which certain ideas and emotions and actions are of God, and their opposites are of Lucifer. It is as impossible for most men to conceive of a morality without sin as of an earth without 'sky'. Since 1692 a great but superficial change has wiped out God's beard and the Devil's horns, but the world is still gripped between two diametrically opposed absolutes. The concept of unity, in which positive and negative are attributes of the same force, in which good and evil are relative, ever-changing, and always joined to the same phenomenon – such a concept is still reserved to the physical sciences and to the few who have grasped the history of ideas. When it is recalled that until the Christian era the underworld was never regarded as a hostile area, that all gods were useful and essentially friendly to man despite occasional lapses; when we see the steady and methodical inculcation into humanity of the idea of man's worthlessness – until redeemed – the necessity of the Devil may become evident as a weapon, a weapon designed and used time and time again in every age to whip men into a surrender to a particular church or church-state.

Our difficulty in believing the – for want of a better word – political inspiration of the Devil is due in great part to the fact that he is called up and damned not only by our social antagonists but by our own side, whatever it may be. The Catholic Church, through its Inquisition, is famous for cultivating Lucifer as the arch-fiend, but the Church's enemies relied no less upon the Old Boy to keep the human mind enthralled. Luther was himself accused of alliance with

4 **superficial**: *oberflächig* 6 **diametrically opposed**: the exact opposite of each other **absolute** (n): sth. that cannot be affected by anything **unity**: harmony 7 **attribute**: *Merkmal* 10 **grasp**: (here) understand **history of ideas**: *Geistesgeschichte* 11 **era**: a period of time in history 12 **hostile**: aggressive; like an enemy **essentially**: basically 13 **lapse**: small mistake 14 **inculcation**: making sb. learn and never forget sth. 15 **redeem**: (here) free sb. from evil powers 16 **evident**: clear 17 **surrender to sth.** (n): giving yourself up to sth. 19 **for want of sth.**: because you do not have sth. 20 **be due to sth.**: be caused by 20–21 **call sb. up**: ask sb. to appear 21 **antagonist**: sb. who works against you 23 **Inquisition**: persecution of people who believe things that the church does not like **arch-fiend**: greatest enemy 24 **Old Boy**: (here) the devil 24–25 **keep sth. enthralled**: hold sth's attention

Hell, and he in turn accused his enemies. To complicate matters further, he believed that he had had contact with the Devil and had argued theology with him. I am not surprised at this, for at my own university a professor of history – a Lutheran, by the way – used to assemble his graduate students, draw the shades, and commune in the classroom with Erasmus. He was never, to my knowledge, officially scoffed at for this, the reason being that the university officials, like most of us, are the children of a history which still sucks at the Devil's teats. At this writing, only England has held back before the temptations of contemporary diabolism. In the countries of the Communist ideology, all resistance of any import is linked to the totally malign capitalist succubi, and in America any man who is not reactionary in his views is open to the charge of alliance with the Red hell. Political opposition, thereby, is given an inhumane overlay which then justifies the abrogation of all normally applied customs of civilized intercourse. A political policy is equated with moral right, and opposition to it with diabolical malevolence. Once such an equation is effectively made, society becomes a congerie of plots and counterplots, and the main role of government changes from that of the arbiter to that of the scourge of God.

The results of this process are no different now from what they ever were, except sometimes in the degree of cruelty inflicted, and not always even in that department. Normally the actions and deeds of a man were all that society felt comfortable in judging. The secret

5 **graduate student**: student in an advanced course of study at college or university **draw the shades**: pull the curtains 6 **Erasmus**: Erasmus of Rotterdam, important Dutch thinker and Catholic priest (1466–1536) 9 **suck at sb.'s teats**: drink milk from sb.'s breast, (here: be strongly influenced by sb.) 10 **contemporary**: belonging to the present time 11 **import** (fml): importance 12 **malign**: with evil intentions **succubus (pl. succubi):** female devil 13 **reactionary**: with older ideas 14 **Red hell** (derog.): Communist countries **inhumane**: cruel to other people **overlay**: (here) appearance 15 **abrogation**: end 16 **intercourse**: (here) communication **equate sth. with sth.**: say that sth. is the same as sth. else 17 **malevolence**: evil intentions 18 **congerie of sth.**: lots of sth. in one place **plot**: secret plan 19 **counterplot**: plot that is a reaction to another plot 20 **arbiter**: person who finds a solution to an argument **scourge**: sb. or sth. that hurts sb. else very much 22 **inflict sth.**: do sth. cruel

intent of an action was left to the ministers, priests, and rabbis to deal with. When diabolism rises, however, actions are the least important manifests of the true nature of a man. The Devil, as Reverend Hale said, is a wily one, and, until an hour before he fell, even God thought him beautiful in Heaven.

The analogy, however, seems to falter when one considers that, while there were no witches then, there are Communists and capitalists now, and in each camp there is certain proof that spies of each side are at work undermining the other. But this is a snobbish objection and not at all warranted by the facts. I have no doubt that people *were* communing with, and even worshipping, the Devil in Salem, and if the whole truth could be known in this case, as it is in others, we should discover a regular and conventionalized propitiation of the dark spirit. One certain evidence of this is the confession of Tituba, the slave of Reverend Parris, and another is the behaviour of the children who were known to have indulged in sorceries with her.

There are accounts of similar *klatsches* in Europe, where the daughters of the towns would assemble at night and, sometimes with fetishes, sometimes with a selected young man, give themselves to love, with some bastardly results. The Church, sharpeyed as it must be when gods long dead are brought to life, condemned these orgies as witchcraft and interpreted them, rightly, as a resurgence of the Dionysiac forces it had crushed long before. Sex, sin, and the Devil were early linked, and so they continued to be in Salem, and are today. From all accounts there are no more puritanical mores in the world than those enforced by the Communists in Russia, where

1 **intent** (fml): intention 4 **wily**: clever 6 **falter**: become weak 9 **undermine sb.**: work against sb. 10 **objection**: statement that you are against sth. or think it is untrue **warranted**: justified 11 **commune with sb.**: have contact with sb. 13 **conventionalize**: become the usual way of doing sth. 14 **propitiation**: making sb. who is angry with you feel less angry 15 **confession**: admission that you have done sth. wrong 16 **indulge in sth.**: (here) enjoy doing sth. that is forbidden 17 **sorcery**: magic 18 **klatsch**: gossip 20 **fetish**: (here) object thought to have magical powers 21 **bastardly results**: (here) children born to unmarried young women 23 **orgy**: wild party, often sexual **resurgence**: return 24 **Dionysiac**: hedonistic 26 **puritanical**: with very strict moral rules **mores**: *Sitten* 27 **enforce sth.**: make sure that sth. (e.g. law, rule) is kept

women's fashions, for instance, are as prudent and all-covering as any American Baptist would desire. The divorce laws lay a tremendous responsibility on the father for the care of his children. Even the laxity of divorce regulations in the early years of the revolution was undoubtedly a revulsion from the nineteenth-century Victorian immobility of marriage and the consequent hypocrisy that developed from it. If for no other reasons, a state so powerful, so jealous of the uniformity of its citizens, cannot long tolerate the atomization of the family. And yet, in American eyes at least, there remains the conviction that the Russian attitude toward women is lascivious. It is the Devil working again, just as he is working within the Slav who is shocked at the very idea of a woman's disrobing herself in a burlesque show. Our opposites are always robed in sexual sin, and it is from this unconscious conviction that demonology gains both its attractive sensuality and its capacity to infuriate and frighten.

Coming into Salem now, Reverend Hale conceives of himself much as a young doctor on his first call. His painfully acquired armoury of symptoms, catchwords, and diagnostic procedures are now to be put to use at last. The road from Beverly is unusually busy this morning, and he has passed a hundred rumours that make him

1 **prudent**: sensible 2 **Baptist**: member of a specific branch of the Protestant church 3 **tremendous**: very large 4 **laxity**: relaxed nature 5 **revulsion**: (here) strong reaction against sth. 6 **immobility**: state of not moving **consequent**: resulting 8 **jealous of sth.** ['dʒeləs]: (here) protecting sth. that is very important to you **uniformity**: all members of a group being the same 9 **atomization of sth.**: breaking sth. up into very small pieces 11 **lascivious** [lə'sɪviəs]: full of sexual desire 12 **Slav** (derog.): sb. from a Slavic country; (here) Russian **disrobe oneself**: get undressed 13 **burlesque show**: performance involving music and sexual dancing **robed in sth.**: (here) wrapped up in sth. and thus hidden 15 **demonology**: study of evil creatures such as demons (*Dämonen*) **sensuality**: *Sinnlichkeit* 18 **infuriate**: make very angry call (n): (here) doctor's visit to a sick person 19 **armoury**: all the weapons one has to fight a battle **catchword**: word that is important in a certain situation **diagnostic** procedure: actions taken to find out more about the true nature of sth.

smile at the ignorance of the yeomanry in this most precise science. He feels himself allied with the best minds of Europe – kings, philosophers, scientists, and ecclesiasts of all churches. His goal is light, goodness and its preservation, and he knows the exaltation of the blessed whose intelligence, sharpened by minute examinations of enormous tracts, is finally called upon to face what may be a bloody fight with the Fiend himself.

[*He appears loaded down with half a dozen heavy books.*]

HALE: Pray you, someone take these!

PARRIS [*delighted*]: Mr Hale! Oh! it's good to see you again! [*Taking some books*]: My, they're heavy!

HALE [*setting down his books*]: They must be; they are weighted with authority.

PARRIS [*a little seared*]: Well, you do come prepared!

HALE: We shall need hard study if it comes to tracking down the Old Boy. [*Noticing* REBECCA] You cannot be Rebecca Nurse?

REBECCA: I am, sir. Do you know me?

HALE: It's strange how I knew you, but I suppose you look as such a good soul should. We have all heard of your great charities in Beverly.

PARRIS: Do you know this gentleman? Mr Thomas Putnam. And his good wife Ann.

HALE: Putnam! I had not expected such distinguished company, sir.

1 **yeomanry** ['jəʊmənri]: class of farmers who own their land 3 **ecclesiast** [ɪˌkliːzi'æst]: person working for the church 4 **preservation**: (here) survival **exaltation**: great happiness 5 **the blessed** ['blesɪd]: holy people **minute** (adj) [maɪ'njuːt]: very small 6 **tract**: (here) document of ideas (often religious) 7 **the Fiend**: the devil 15 **track sb. down**: pursue sb. until you have found them 23 **distinguished**: highly respected **company**: (here) people together with other people

PUTNAM [*phased*]: It does not seem to help us today, Mr Hale. We look to you to come to our house and save our child.

HALE: Your child ails too?

MRS PUTNAM: Her soul, her soul seems flown away. She sleeps and yet she walks ...

PUTNAM: She cannot eat.

HALE: Cannot eat! [*Thinks on it. Then, to* PROCTOR *and* GILES COREY] Do you men have afflicted children?

PARRIS: No, no, these are farmers. John Proctor –

GILES COREY: He don't believe in witches.

PROCTOR [*to* HALE]: I never spoke on witches one way or the other. Will you come, Giles?

GILES: No – no, John, I think not. I have some few queer questions of my own to ask this fellow.

PROCTOR: I've heard you to be a sensible man, Mr Hale. I hope you'll leave some of it in Salem.
[PROCTOR *goes*. HALE *stands embarrassed for an instant*.]

PARRIS [*quickly*]: Will you look at my daughter, sir? [*Leads* HALE *to the bed*.] She has tried to leap out the window; we discovered her this morning on the highroad, waving her arms as though she'd fly.

HALE [*narrowing his eyes*]: Tries to fly.

PUTNAM: She cannot bear to hear the Lord's name, Mr Hale; that's a sure sign of witchcraft afloat.

HALE [*holding up his hands*]: No, no. Now let me instruct you. We cannot look to superstitition in this. The Devil is precise; the marks of his presence are definite as stone, and I must tell you all

13 **queer** (old-fashioned): strange 20 **highroad**: the main road of a town or village
24 **afloat**: being around 27 **definite**: clear to see

that I shall not proceed unless you are prepared to believe me if I should find no bruise of hell upon her.

PARRIS: It is agreed, sir – it is agreed – we will abide by your judgement.

HALE: Good then. [*He goes to the bed, looks down at* BETTY. *To* PARRIS] Now, sir, what were your first warning of this strangeness?

PARRIS: Why, sir – I discovered her [*indicating* ABIGAIL] – and my niece and ten or twelve of the other girls, dancing in the forest last night.

HALE [*surprised*]: You permit dancing?

PARRIS: No, no, it were secret –

MRS PUTNAM [*unable to wait*]: Mr Parris's slave has knowledge of conjurin', sir.

PARRIS [*to* MRS PUTNAM]: We cannot be sure of that, Goody Ann –

MRS PUTNAM [*frightened, very softly*]: I know it, sir. I sent my child – she should learn from Tituba who murdered her sisters.

REBECCA [*horrrfied*]: Goody Ann! You sent a child to conjure up the dead?

MRS PUTNAM: Let God blame me, not you, not you, Rebecca! I'll not have you judging me any morel [*To* HALE] Is it a natural work to lose seven children before they live a day?

PARRIS: Sssh!

[REBECCA, *with great pain, turns her face away. There is a pause.*]

HALE: Seven dead in childbirth.

MRS PUTNAM [*softly*]: Aye. [*Her voice breaks; she looks up at him. Silence.* HALE *is impressed.* PARRIS *looks to him. He goes to his books, opens one, turns pages, then reads. All wait, avidly.*]

2 **bruise**: (here) a mark, a sign 3 **abide by sth.**: accept sth. 20 **Is it a natural work?**: Does it have natural causes? 27 **avidly**: eagerly; very interested

PARRIS [*hushed*]: What book is that?

MRS PUTNAM: What's there, sir?

HALE [*with a tasty love of intellectual pursuit*]: Here is all the invisible world, caught, defined, and calculated. In these books the Devil stands stripped of all his brute disguises. Here are all your familiar spirits – your incubi and succubi; your witches that go by land, by air, and by sea; your wizards of the night and of the day. Have no fear now – we shall find him out if he has come among us, and I mean to crush him utterly if he has shown his face! [*He starts for the bed.*]

REBECCA: Will it hurt the child, sir?

HALE: I cannot tell. If she is truly in the Devil's grip we may have to rip and tear to get her free.

REBECCA: I think I'll go, then. I am too old for this. [*She rises.*]

PARRIS [*striving for conviction*]: Why, Rebecca, we may open up the boil of all our troubles today!

REBECCA: Let us hope for that. I go to God for you, sir.

PARRIS [*with trepidation – and resentment*]: I hope you do not mean we go to Satan here I [*Slight pause.*]

REBECCA: I wish I knew. [*She goes out; they feel resentful of her note of moral superiority.*]

PUTNAM [*abruptly*]: Come, Mr Hale, let's get on. Sit you here.

3 **tasty**: (here) enjoying sth. greatly **intellectual pursuit**: studying an academic topic 5 **strip sb. of sth.**: take sth. away from sb. **brute**: rough, unpleasant **disguise**: *Verschleierung* 6 **incubus, pl. incubi**: male devil 7 **wizard**: man who can do magic 9 **utterly**: completely 13 **rip**: pull very strongly **tear** (v) **[teə(r)]**: (here) remove sth. from sth. else by pulling hard 15 **strive for**: work very hard to achieve sth. 16 **boil** (n): *Eiterbeule, (hier: Ursache allen Übels)* 21 **superiority**: feeling that you are better than others

GILES: Mr Hale, I have always wanted to ask a learned man what signifies the readin' of strange books?

HALE: What books?

GILES: I cannot tell; she hides them.

HALE: Who does this?

GILES: Martha, my wife. I have waked at night many a time and found her in a corner, readin' of a book. Now what do you make of that?

HALE: Why, that's not necessarily –

GILES: It discomforts me! Last night – mark this – I tried and tried and could not say my prayers. And then she closes her book and walks out of the house, and suddenly – mark this – I could pray again!

Old Giles must be spoken for, if only because his fate was to be so remarkable and so different from that of all the others. He was in his early eighties at this time, and was the most comical hero in the history. No man has ever been blamed for so much. If a cow was missed, the first thought was to look for her around Corey's house; a fire blazing up at night brought suspicion of arson to his door. He didn't give a hoot for public opinion, and only in his last years – after he had married Martha – did he bother much with the church. That she stopped his prayer is very probable, but he forgot to say that he'd only recently learned any prayers and it didn't take much to make him stumble over them. He was a crank and a nuisance, but

1 **learned** ['lɜːnɪd]: knowing a lot from having studied a lot 1–2 **what signifies ...?** (old use): what does ... mean? 10 **discomfort sb.**: make sb. feel uncomfortable 14 **speak for sb.**: defend sb. 16–17 **the history**: (here) the historical background to this story 19 **blaze up**: burn **arson**: purposefully burning sth. down 20 **not give a hoot for sth.**: not care at all about sth. 21 **bother with sth.** (v): care about sth. 23 **it didn't take much**: it was done very easily 24 **crank**: person who gets upset easily **nuisance** ['njuːsns]: sb. or sth. that annoys people

withal a deeply innocent and brave man. In court, once, he was asked if it were true that he had been frightened by the strange behaviour of a hog and had then said he knew it to be the Devil in an animal's shape. 'What frighted you?' he was asked. He forgot everything but the word 'frighted', and instantly replied, 'I do not know that I ever spoke that word in my life.'

HALE: Ah! The stoppage of prayer – that is strange. I'll speak further on that with you.

GILES: I'm not sayin' she's touched the Devil, now, but I'd admire to know what books she reads and why she hides them. She'll not answer me, y' see.

HALE: Aye, we'll discuss it. [*To all*] Now mark me, if the Devil is in her you will witness some frightful wonders in this room, so please to keep your wits about you. Mr Putnam, stand close in case she flies. Now, Betty, dear, will you sit up? [PUTNAM *comes in closer, ready-handed.* HALE *sits* BETTY *up, but she hangs limp in his hands.*] Hmmm. [*He observes her carefully. The others watch breathlessly.*] Can you hear me? I am John Hale, minister of Beverly. I have come to help you, dear. Do you remember my two little girls in Beverly?
[*She does not stir in his hands.*]

PARRIS [*in fright*]: How can it be the Devil? Why would he choose my house to strike? We have all manner of licentious people in the village!

HALE: What victory would the Devil have to win a soul already bad? It is the best the Devil wants, and who is better than the minister?

GILES: That's deep, Mr Parris, deep, deep!

1 **withal** [wɪθ'ɔːl]: all in all 3 **hog**: pig 7 **stoppage**: stopping 9 **admire to do sth.** (old use): feeling a strong wish to do sth. 11 **y'see**: you see 13 **frightful**: terrible 14 **keep your wits about you**: keep thinking clearly 16 **ready-handed**: ready to react if one has to **limp**: without any strength 23 **strike sth.**: (here) attack sth. **licentious**: with bad morals

PARRIS [*with resolution now*]: Betty! Answer Mr Hale! Betty!

HALE: Does someone afflict you, child? It need not be a woman, mind you, or a man. Perhaps some bird invisible to others comes to you – perhaps a pig, a mouse, or any beast at all. Is there some figure bids you fly? [*The child remains limp in his hands. In silence he lays her back on the pillow. Now, holding out his hands toward her, he intones.*] In nomine Domini Sabaoth sui filiique ite ad infernos. [*She does not stir. He turns to* ABIGAIL, *his eyes narrowing.*] Abigail, what sort of dancing were you doing with her in the forest?

ABIGAIL: Why – common dancing is all.

PARRIS: I think I ought to say that I – I saw a kettle in the grass where they were dancing.

ABIGAIL: That were only soup.

HALE: What sort of soup were in this kettle, Abigail?

ABIGAIL: Why, it were beans – and lentils, I think, and –

HALE: Mr Parris, you did not notice, did you, any living thing in the kettle? A mouse, perhaps, a spider, a frog – ?

PARRIS [*fearfully*]: I – do believe there were some movement – in the soup.

ABIGAIL: That jumped in, we never put it in!

HALE [*quickly*]: What jumped in?

ABIGAIL: Why, a very little frog jumped –

PARRIS: A frog, Abby!

HALE [*grasping* ABIGAIL]: Abigail, it may be your cousin is dying. Did you call the Devil last night?

1 **with resolution**: firmly 7 **intone**: say sth. seriously, with a firm voice 7–8 **In nomine Domini ... ite ad infernos**: “In the name of the Lord Sabaoth and his son, go (back) to hell.” 11 **common dancing is all** (old use): normal dancing, and that is all 15 **kettle**: metal pot in which you cook soup, etc. 16 **lentil**: *Linse*

ABIGAIL: I never called him! Tituba, Tituba …

PARRIS [*blanched*]: She called the Devil?

HALE: I should like to speak with Tituba.

PARRIS: Goody Ann, will you bring her up?
[MRS PUTNAM *exits.*]

HALE: How did she call him?

ABIGAIL: I know not – she spoke Barbados.

HALE: Did you feel any strangeness when she called him? A sudden cold wind, perhaps? A trembling below the ground?

ABIGAIL: I didn't see no Devil! [*Shaking* BETTY] Betty, wake up. Betty! Betty!

HALE: You cannot evade me, Abigail. Did your cousin drink any of the brew in that kettle?

ABIGAIL: She never drank it!

HALE: Did you drink it?

ABIGAIL: No, sir!

HALE: Did Tituba ask you to drink it?

ABIGAIL: She tried, but I refused.

HALE: Why are you concealing? Have you sold yourself to Lucifer?

ABIGAIL: I never sold myself! I'm a good girl! I'm a proper girl!
[MRS PUTNAM *enters with* TITUBA, *and instantly* ABIGAIL *points at* TITUBA.]

ABIGAIL: She made me do it! She made Betty do it!

2 **blanched**: gone white in the face 5 **exit** (v): leave (a theatre stage) 7 **Barbados**: an island in the Caribbean 12 **evade sb.**: get away from sb. 13 **brew**: drink that has been boiled and mixed with several ingredients 19 **conceal**: hide sth.
20 **proper**: sticking by the rules

TITUBA [*shocked and angry*]: Abby!

ABIGAIL: She makes me drink blood!

PARRIS: Blood!!

MRS PUTNAM: My baby's blood?

TITUBA: No, no, chicken blood. I give she chicken blood!

HALE: Woman, have you enlisted these children for the Devil?

TITUBA: No, no, sir, I don't truck with no Devil!

HALE: Why can she not wake? Are you silencing this child?

TITUBA: I love me Betty!

HALE: You have sent your spirit out upon this child, have you not? Are you gathering souls for the Devil?

ABIGAIL: She sends her spirit on me in church; she makes me laugh at prayer!

PARRIS: She have often laughed at prayer!

ABIGAIL: She comes to me every night to go and drink blood!

TITUBA: You beg me to conjure! She beg *me* make charm –

ABIGAIL: Don't lie! [*To* HALE]: She comes to me while I sleep; she's always making me dream corruptions!

TITUBA: Why you say that, Abby?

ABIGAIL: Sometimes I wake and find myself standing in the open doorway and not a stitch on my body! I always hear her laughing in my sleep. I hear her singing her Barbados songs and tempting me with –

TITUBA: Mister Reverend, I never –

6 **enlist sb. for sth.**: convince sb. to become a part of sth. 7 **truck with sb.** (old use): deal with sb. 8 **silence sb.**: stop sb. from speaking 9 **me**: (here) my
11 **gather**: collect 21 **not a stitch on my body**: completely naked

HALE [*resolved now*]: Tituba, I want you to wake this child.

TITUBA: I have no power on this child, sir.

HALE: You most certainly do, and you will free her from it now! When did you compact with the Devil?

TITUBA: I don't compact with no Devil!

PARRIS: You will confess yourself or I will take you out and whip you to your death, Tituba!

PUTNAM: This woman must be hanged! She must be taken and hanged!

TITUBA [*terrified, falls to her knees*]: No, no, don't hang Tituba! I tell him I don't desire to work for him, sir.

PARRIS: The Devil?

HALE: Then you saw him! [TITUBA *weeps*.] Now Tituba, I know that when we bind ourselves to Hell it is very hard to break with it. We are going to help you tear yourself free –

TITUBA [*frightened by the coming process*]: Mister Reverend, I do believe somebody else be witchin' these children.

HALE: Who?

TITUBA: I don't know, sir, but the Devil got him numerous witches.

HALE: Does he! [*It is a clue.*] Tituba, look into my eyes. Come, look into me.
[*She raises her eyes to his fearfully.*]
You would be a good Christian woman, would you not, Tituba?

TITUBA: Aye, sir, a good Christian woman.

HALE: And you love these little children?

2 **have power on sb.** (old use): have power over sb. 4 **compact with sb.** (v): having contact with sb. 13 **weep**: cry 14 **bind yourself to sth.**: connect yourself to sth. 17 **witch sb.**: use magic on sb. 20 **clue**: hint

TITUBA: Oh, yes, sir, I don't desire to hurt little children.

HALE: And you love God, Tituba?

TITUBA: I love God with all my bein'.

HALE: Now, in God's holy name –

TITUBA: Bless Him. Bless Him. [*She is rocking on her knees, sobbing in terror.*]

HALE: And to His glory –

TITUBA: Eternal glory. Bless Him – bless God …

HALE: Open yourself, Tituba – open yourself and let God's holy light shine on you.

TITUBA: Oh, bless the Lord.

HALE: When the Devil comes to you does he ever come – with another person?
[*She stares up into his face.*]
Perhaps another person in the village? Someone you know.

PARRIS: Who came with him?

PUTNAM: Sarah Good? Did you ever see Sarah Good with him? Or Osburn?

PARRIS: Was it man or woman came with him?

TITUBA: Man or woman. Was – was woman.

PARRIS: What woman? A woman, you said. What woman?

TITUBA: It was black dark, and I –

PARRIS: You could see him, why could you not see her?

TITUBA: Well, they was always talking; they was always runnin' round and carryin' on –

5 **rock** (v): move back and forth **sob**: cry loudly

PARRIS: You mean out of Salem? Salem witches?

TITUBA: I believe so, yes, sir.
[*Now* HALE *takes her hand. She is surprised.*]

HALE: Tituba. You must have no fear to tell us who they are, do you understand? We will protect you. The Devil can never overcome a minister. You know that, do you not?

TITUBA [*kisses* HALE'S *hand*]: Aye, sir, oh, I do.

HALE: You have confessed yourself to witchcraft, and that speaks a wish to come to Heaven's side. And we will bless you, Tituba.

TITUBA [*deeply relieved*]: Oh, God bless you, Mr Hale!

HALE [*with rising exaltation*]: You are God's instrument put in our hands to discover the Devil's agents among us. You are selected, Tituba, you are chosen to help us cleanse our village. So speak utterly, Tituba, turn your back on him and face God – face God, Tituba, and God will protect you.

TITUBA [*joining with him*]: Oh, God, protect Tituba!

HALE [*kindly*]: Who came to you with the Devil? Two? Three? Four? How many?
[TITUBA *pants, and begins rocking back and forth again, staring ahead.*]

TITUBA: There was four. There was four.

PARRIS [*pressing in on her*]: Who? Who? Their names, their names!

TITUBA [*suddenly bursting out*]: Oh, how many times he bid me kill you, Mr Parris!

PARRIS: Kill me!

5–6 **overcome sb.**: beat sb. in a fight 8 **confess oneself to sth.**: admit having done sth. 12 **agent**: person who does sb. else's work 13 **cleanse**: make clean 14 **utterly** (old-fashioned): openly 19 **pant** (v): breathe heavily

TITUBA [*in a fury*]: He say Mr Parris must be kill! Mr Parris no goodly man, Mr Parris mean man and no gentle man, and he bid me rise out of my bed and cut your throat! [*They gasp.*] But I tell him 'No! I don't hate that man. I don't want kill that man.' But he say, 'You work for me, Tituba, and I make you free! I give you pretty dress to wear, and put you way high up in the air, and you gone fly back to Barbados!' And I say, 'You lie, Devil, you lie!' And then he come one stormy night to me, and he say, 'Look! I have white people belong to me.' And I look – and there was Goody Good.

PARRIS: Sarah Good!

TITUBA [*rocking and weeping*]: Aye, sir, and Goody Osburn.

MRS PUTNAM: I knew it! Goody Osburn were midwife to me three times. I begged you, Thomas, did I not? I begged him not to call Osburn because I feared her. My babies always shrivelled in her hands!

HALE: Take courage, you must give us all their names. How can you bear to see this child suffering? Look at her, Tituba. [*He is indicating* BETTY *on the bed.*] Look at her God-given innocence; her soul is so tender; we must protect her, Tituba; the Devil is out and preying on her like a beast upon the flesh of the pure lamb. God will bless you for your help.
[ABIGAIL *rises, staring as though inspired, and cries out.*]

ABIGAIL: I want to open myself!
[*They turn to her, startled. She is enraptured, as though in a pearly light.*]

1 **... Mr Parris must be kill**: ... Mr Parris must be killed 2 **goodly**: morally good 6–7 **you gone fly back to ...**: you are going to fly back to ... 8–9 **I have white people belong to me**: white people belong to me 13 **midwife**: sb. who helps women with childbirth 19 **innocence**: state of not being guilty of something 20 **tender**: soft, easily damaged 21 **prey on sb.**: (here) take advantage of sb. weaker than you 25 **enraptured**: very happy **pearly**: milky-white, like a pearl

I want the light of God, I want the sweet love of Jesus! I danced for the Devil; I saw him; I wrote in his book; I go back to Jesus; I kiss His hand. I saw Sarah Good with the Devil! I saw Goody Osburn with the Devil! I saw Bridget Bishop with the Devil! [*As she is speaking,* BETTY *is rising from the bed, a fever in her eyes, and picks up the chant.*]

BETTY [*staring too*]: I saw George Jacobs with the Devil! I saw Goody Howe with the Devil!

PARRIS: She speaks! [*He rushes to embrace* BETTY.] She speaks!

HALE: Glory to God! It is broken, they are free!

BETTY [*calling out hysterically and with great relief*]: I saw Martha Bellows with the Devil!

ABIGAIL: I saw Goody Sibber with the Devil! [*It is rising to a great glee.*]

PUTNAM: The marshal, I'll call the marshal!

[PARRIS *is shouting a peer of thanksgiving.*]

BETTY: I saw Alice Barrow with the Devil! [*The curtain begins to fall.*]

HALE [*as* PUTNAM *goes out*]: Let the marshal bring irons!

ABIGAIL: I saw Goody Hawkins with the Devil!

BETTY: I saw Goody Bibber with the Devil!

ABIGAIL: I saw Goody Booth with the Devil!
On their ecstatic cries

THE CURTAIN FALLS

6 **pick up a chant**: join in a song 9 **embrace sb.**: hug sb. 14 **glee**: happiness
19 **irons**: old-fashioned handcuffs 23 **ecstatic**: crazy with happiness

ACT TWO

The common room of Proctor's house, eight days later.

At the right is a door opening on the fields outside. A fireplace is at the left, and behind it a stairway leading upstairs. It is the low, dark, and rather long living-room of the time. As the curtain rises, the room is empty. From above, ELIZABETH *is heard softly singing to the children. Presently the door opens and* JOHN PROCTOR *enters, carrying his gun. He glances about the room as he comes toward the fireplace, then halts for an instant as he hears her singing. He continues on to the fireplace, leans the gun against the wall as be swings a pot out of the fire and smells it. Then he lifts out the ladle and tastes. He is not quite pleased. He reaches to a cupboard, takes a pinch of salt, and drops it into the pot. As he is tasting again, her footsteps are heard on the stair. He swings the pot into the fireplace and goes to a basin and washes his hands and face.* ELIZABETH *enters.*

ELIZABETH: What keeps you so late? It's almost dark.

PROCTOR: I were planting far out to the forest edge.

ELIZABETH: Oh, you're done then.

PROCTOR: Aye, the farm is seeded. The boys asleep?

ELIZABETH: They will be soon. [*And she goes to the fireplace, proceeds to ladle up stew in a dish.*]

PROCTOR: Pray now for a fair summer.

ELIZABETH: Aye.

PROCTOR: Are you well today?

1 **common room**: living room 5 **presently**: now 6 **glance**: look 9 **swing a pot out of the fire**: pull a pot away from the fire 10 **ladle**: large spoon, used for serving soup 11 **pinch of salt**: tiny amount of salt 18 **seed** (v): plant seeds (*Samen*) (in an area of land) 20 **ladle up sth.**: serve sth. **stew**: *Eintopf*

ELIZABETH: I am. [*She brings the plate to the table, and, indicating the food*] It is a rabbit.

PROCTOR [*going to the table*]: Oh, is it! In Jonathan's trap?

ELIZABETH: No, she walked into the house this afternoon; I found her sittin' in the corner like she come to visit.

PROCTOR: Oh, that's a good sign walkin' in.

ELIZABETH: Pray God. It hurt my heart to strip her, poor rabbit. [*She sits and watches him taste it.*]

PROCTOR: It's well seasoned.

ELIZABETH [*blushing with pleasure*]: I took great care. She's tender?

PROCTOR: Aye. [*He eats. She watches him.*] I think we'll see green fields soon. It's warm as blood beneath the clods.

ELIZABETH: That's well.
[*Proctor eats, then looks up.*]

PROCTOR: If the crop is good I'll buy George Jacob's heifer. How would that please you?

ELIZABETH: Aye, it would.

PROCTOR [*with a grin*]: I mean to please you, Elizabeth.

ELIZABETH [*it is hard to say*]: I know it, John.
[*He gets up, goes to her, kisses her. She receives it. With a certain disappointment, he returns to the table.*]

PROCTOR [*as gently as he can*]: Cider?

1 **indicate**: point to 7 **pray God**: used to express that you hope that sth. is true **strip sth.**: (here): pull the fur off sth. (an animal) 9 **seasoned**: with salt, pepper, etc. (of food) 10 **tender**: soft 12 **clod**: piece of earth 15 **heifer**: young cow

ELIZABETH [*with a sense of reprimanding herself for having forgot*]: Aye! [*She gets up and goes and pours a glass for him. He now arches his back.*]

PROCTOR: This farm's a continent when you go foot by foot droppin' seeds in it.

ELIZABETH [*coming with the cider*]: It must be.

PROCTOR [*drinks a long draught, then, putting the glass down*]: You ought to bring some flowers in the house.

ELIZABETH: Oh, I forgot! I will tomorrow.

PROCTOR: It's winter in here yet. On Sunday let you come with me, and we'll walk the farm together; I never see such a load of flowers on the earth. [*With good feeling he goes and looks up at the sky through the open doorway.*] Lilacs have a purple smell. Lilac is the smell of nightfall, I think. Massachusetts is a beauty in the spring!

ELIZABETH: Aye, it is.

[*There is a pause. She is watching him from the table as he stands there absorbing the night. It is as though she would speak but cannot. Instead, now, she takes up his plate and glass and fork and goes with them to the basin. Her back is turned to him. He turns to her and watches her. A sense of their separation rises.*]

PROCTOR: I think you're sad again. Are you?

ELIZABETH [*she doesn't want friction, and yet she must*]: You come so late I thought you'd gone to Salem this afternoon.

PROCTOR: Why? I have no business in Salem.

ELIZABETH: You did speak of going, earlier this week.

PROCTOR [*he knows what she means*]: I thought better of it since.

1 **reprimand sb.**: tell sb. that they have done sth. wrong 2–3 **arch your back**: bend your back 7 **draught [drɑːft]**: amount of liquid 13 **lilac**: *Flieder* 14 **nightfall**: time when it gets dark at the end of the day 23 **friction**: (here) conflict

ELIZABETH: Mary Warren's there today.

PROCTOR: Why'd you let her? You heard me forbid her go to Salem any more!

ELIZABETH: I couldn't stop her.

PROCTOR [*holding back a full condemnation of her*]: It is a fault, it is a fault, Elizabeth – you're the mistress here, not Mary Warren.

ELIZABETH: She frightened all my strength away.

PROCTOR: How may that mouse frighten you, Elizabeth? You –

ELIZABETH: It is a mouse no more. I forbid her go, and she raises up her chin like the daughter of a prince and says to me, 'I must go to Salem, Goody Proctor; I am an official of the court!'

PROCTOR: Court! What court?

ELIZABETH: Aye, it is a proper court they have now. They've sent four judges out of Boston, she says, weighty magistrates of the General Court, and at the head sits the Deputy Governor of the Province.

PROCTOR [*astonished*]: Why, she's mad.

ELIZABETH: I would to God she were. There be fourteen people in the jail now, she says.
[PROCTOR *simply looks at her, unable to grasp it.*]
And they'll be tried, and the court have power to hang them too, she says.

PROCTOR [*scoffing, but without conviction*]: Ah, they'd never hang –

5 **condemnation**: showing that you think sb. has done sth. wrong **fault**: (here) mistake 6 **mistress** (old-fashioned): woman in charge of a household
14 **weighty** **['weɪti]**: important **magistrate**: (here) judge 15 **sit at the head**: be in charge of an institution or meeting **Deputy**: person who is second in rank after the most important person **Governor**: political leader of a colony in North America 18 **I would to God** (old-fashioned): I wish by God 19 **jail** (AE): prison

ELIZABETH: The Deputy Governor promise hangin' if they'll not confess, John. The town's gone wild, I think. She speak of Abigail, and I thought she were a saint, to hear her. Abigail brings the other girls into the court, and where she walks the crowd will part like the sea for Israel. And folks are brought before them, and if they scream and howl and fall to the floor – the person's clapped in the jail for bewitchin' them.

PROCTOR [*wide-eyed*]: Oh, it is a black mischief.

ELIZABETH: I think you must go to Salem, John.
[*He turns to her.*]
I think so. You must tell them it is a fraud.

PROCTOR [*thinking beyond this*]: Aye, it is, it is surely.

ELIZABETH: Let you go to Ezekiel Cheever – he knows you well. And tell him what she said to you last week in her uncle's house. She said it had naught to do with witchcraft, did she not?

PROCTOR [*in thought*]: Aye, she did, she did.
[*Now, a pause.*]

ELIZABETH [*quietly, fearing to anger him by prodding*]: God forbid you keep that from the court, John. I think they must be told.

PROCTOR [*quietly, struggling with his thought*]: Aye, they must, they must. It is a wonder they do believe her.

ELIZABETH: I would go to Salem now, John – let you go tonight.

PROCTOR: I'll think on it.

ELIZABETH [*with her courage now*]: You cannot keep it, John.

PROCTOR [*angering*]: I know I cannot keep it. I say I will think on it!

ELIZABETH [*hurt, and very coldly*]: Good, then, let you think on it. [*She stands and starts to walk out of the room.*]

5 **part** (v): separate to make a path in the middle 7 **clap sb. in jail** (sl): put sb. in prison 11 **fraud [frɔːd]**: crime of lying in order to get an advantage 18 **prod**: (here) force

PROCTOR: I am only wondering how I may prove what she told me, Elizabeth. If the girl's a saint now, I think it is not easy to prove she's fraud, and the town gone so silly. She told it to me in a room alone – I have no proof for it.

ELIZABETH: You were alone with her?

PROCTOR [*stubbornly*]: For a moment alone, aye.

ELIZABETH: Why, then, it is not as you told me.

PROCTOR [*his anger rising*]: For a moment, I say. The others come in soon after.

ELIZABETH [*quietly – she has suddenly lost all faith in him*]: Do as you wish, then. [*She starts to turn.*]

PROCTOR: Woman.
[*She turns to him.*]
I'll not have your suspicion any more.

ELIZABETH [*a little loftily*]: I have no –

PROCTOR: I'll not have it!

ELIZABETH: Then let you not earn it.

PROCTOR [*with a violent undertone*]: You doubt me yet?

ELIZABETH [*with a smile, to keep her dignity*]: John, if it were not Abigail that you must go to hurt, would you falter now? I think not.

PROCTOR: Now look you –

ELIZABETH: I see what I see, John.

PROCTOR [*with solemn warning*]: You will not judge me more, Elizabeth. I have good reason to think before I charge fraud on Abigail,

2–3 **be fraud** (old use): commit a fraud 6 **stubborn** ['stʌbən]: not willing to change one's mind 14 **I'll not have sth.**: I'm not willing to tolerate sth.
15 **loftily**: in a way that shows you think you are better than other people
20 **falter**: (here) hesitate

and I will think on it. Let you look to your own improvement before you go to judge your husband any more. I have forgot Abigail, and –

ELIZABETH: And I.

PROCTOR: Spare me! You forget nothin' and forgive nothin'. Learn charity, woman. I have gone tiptoe in this house all seven month since she is gone. I have not moved from there to there without I think to please you, and still an everlasting funeral marches round your heart. I cannot speak but I am doubted, every moment judged for lies, as though I come into a court when I come into this house!

ELIZABETH: John, you are not open with me. You saw her with a crowd, you said. Now you –

PROCTOR: I'll plead my honesty no more, Elizabeth.

ELIZABETH [*now she would justify herself*]: John, I am only –

PROCTOR: No more! I should have roared you down when first you told me your suspicion. But I wilted, and, like a Christian, I confessed. Confessed! Some dream I had must have mistaken you for God that day. But you're not, you're not, and let you remember it! Let you look sometimes for the goodness in me, and judge me not.

ELIZABETH: I do not judge you. The magistrate sits in your heart that judges you. I never thought you but a good man, John – [*with a smile*] – only somewhat bewildered.

PROCTOR [*laughing bitterly*]: Oh, Elizabeth, your justice would freeze beer! [*He turns suddenly toward a sound outside. He starts for the door as* MARY WARREN *enters. As soon as he sees her, he goes directly to her and grabs her by her cloak, furious.*] How do you go to

5 **Spare me!**: Stop talking! 6 **charity**: (here) forgiveness 14 **plead**: state formally (usually in court) whether you are guilty or not 16 **roar sb. down**: scream loudly to keep sb. from speaking 17 **wilt**: (here) get weak 18–19 **mistake sb. for sb.**: think wrongly that sb. is sb. else

Salem when I forbid it? Do you mock me? [*Shaking her*] I'll whip you if you dare leave this house again!
[*Strangely, she doesn't resist him, but hangs limply by his grip.*]

MARY WARREN: I am sick, I am sick, Mr Proctor. Pray, pray, hurt me not. [*Her strangeness throws him off, and her evident pallor and weakness. He frees her.*] My insides are all shuddery; I am in the proceedings all day, sir.

PROCTOR [*with draining anger – his curiosity is draining it*]: And what of these proceedings here? When will you proceed to keep this house, as you are paid nine pound a year to do – and my wife not wholly well?
[*As though to compensate,* MARY WARREN *goes to* ELIZABETH *with a small rag doll.*]

MARY WARREN: I made a gift for you today, Good Proctor. I had to sit long hours in a chair, and passed the time with sewing.

ELIZABETH [*perplexed, looking at the doll*]: Why, thank you, it's a fair poppet.

MARY WARREN [*with a trembling, decayed voice*]: We must all love each other now, Goody Proctor.

ELIZABETH [*amazed at her strangeness*]: Aye, indeed we must.

MARY WARREN [*glancing at the room*]: I'll get up early in the morning and clean the house. I must sleep now. [*She turns and starts off.*]

PROCTOR: Mary.
[*She halts.*]
Is it true? There be fourteen women arrested?

MARY WARREN: No, sir. There be thirty-nine now – [*She suddenly breaks off and sobs and sits down, exhausted.*]

1 **mock sb.**: make fun of sb. 5 **pallor** ['pælə(r)]: paleness in the face 6 **shuddery**: trembling 7 **proceedings**: (here) court trial 8 **draining**: getting weaker
12 **compensate**: make up for sth. bad 13 **rag doll**: doll made from pieces of cloth
16 **perplexed**: confused 17 **poppet** (old-fashioned): doll 18 **decayed**: (here) weak 22 **start off**: start to leave

ELIZABETH: Why, she's weepin'! What ails you, child?

MARY WARREN: Goody Osburn – will hang!
[*There is a shocked pause, while she sobs.*]

PROCTOR: Hang! [*He calls into her face.*] Hang, y'say?

MARY WARREN [*through her weeping*]: Aye.

PROCTOR: The Deputy Governor will permit it?

MARY WARREN: He sentenced her. He must. [*To ameliorate it.*] But not Sarah Good. For Sarah Good confessed, y'see.

PROCTOR: Confessed! To what?

MARY WARREN: That she – [*in horror at the memory*] – she sometimes made a compact with Lucifer, and wrote her name in his black book – with her blood – and bound herself to torment Christians till God's thrown down – and we all must worship Hell forevermore.
[*Pause.*]

PROCTOR: But – surely you know what a jabberer she is. Did you tell them that?

MARY WARREN: Mr Proctor, in open court she near to choked us all to death.

PROCTOR: How, choked you?

MARY WARREN: She sent her spirit out.

ELIZABETH: Oh, Mary, Mary, surely you –

MARY WARREN [*with an indignant edge*]: She tried to kill me many times, Goody Proctor!

ELIZABETH: Why, I never heard you mention that before.

7 **sentence sb.**: give sb. an official punishment in court **ameliorate sth.** [əˈmiːliəreɪt]: make sth. better 12 **torment** [ˈtɔːment]: make sb. suffer 16 **jabberer**: person who talks a lot and is not taken seriously 20 **choke sb.**: make sb. stop breathing 23 **indignant**: angry because you feel treated unfairly

MARY WARREN: I never knew it before. I never knew anything before. When she come into the court I say to myself, I must not accuse this woman, for she sleep in ditches, and so very old and poor. But then – then she sit there, denying and denying, and I feel a misty coldness climbin' up my back, and the skin on my skull begin to creep, and I feel a clamp around my neck and I cannot breathe air; and then – [*entranced*] – I hear a voice, a screamin' voice, and it were my voice – and all at once I remembered everything she done to me!

PROCTOR: Why? What did she do to you?

MARY WARREN [*like one awakened to a marvellous secret insight*]: So many time, Mr Proctor, she come to this very door, beggin' bread and a cup of cider – and mark this: whenever I turned her away empty, she *mumbled*.

ELIZABETH: Mumbled! She may mumble if she's hungry.

MARY WARREN: But what does she mumble? You must remember, Goody Proctor. Last month – a Monday, I think she walked away, and I thought my guts would burst for two days after. Do you remember it?

ELIZABETH: Why – I do, I think, but –

MARY WARREN: And so I told that to Judge Hathome, and he asks her so. 'Goody Osburn,' says he, 'what curse do you mumble that this girl must fall sick after turning you away?' And then she replies – [*mimicking an old crone*] – 'Why, your excellence, no curse at all. I only say my commandments; I hope I may say my commandments,' says she!

3 **ditch**: *Graben* 5 **misty**: slightly wet 5–6 **my skin ... begin(s) to creep**: *ich bekomme eine Gänsehaut* 6 **skull**: bones in the head **clamp**: tool that holds two things firmly together 7 **entranced**: completely absorbed 11 **awakened to sth.**: (here) noticing sth. for the first time **insight**: understanding 18 **guts**: *Eingeweide* 24 **mimic sb.**: copy sb.'s way of speaking **crone** (derog.): old woman **your excellence**: form of addressing sb. in a high position 25 **commandment**: God's law (esp. in the Ten Commandments given to Moses)

ELIZABETH: And that's an upright answer.

MARY WARREN: Aye, but then Judge Hathorne say, 'Recite for us your commandments!' – [*leaning avidly toward them*] and of all the ten she could not say a single one. She never knew no commandments, and they had her in a flat lie!

PROCTOR: And so condemned her?

MARY WARREN [*now a little strained, seeing his stubborn doubt*]: Why, they must when she condemned herself.

PROCTOR: But the proof, the proof!

MARY WARREN [*with greater impatience with him*]: I told you the proof. It's hard proof, hard as rock, the judges said.

PROCTOR [*pauses an instant, then*]: You will not go to court again, Mary Warren.

MARY WARREN: I must tell you, sir, I will be gone every day now. I am amazed you do not see what weighty work we do.

PROCTOR: What work you do! It's strange work for a Christian girl to hang old women!

MARY WARREN: But, Mr Proctor, they will not hang them if they confess. Sarah Good will only sit in jail some time [*recalling*] – and here's a wonder for you; think on this. Goody Good is pregnant!

ELIZABETH: Pregnant! Are they mad? The woman's near to sixty!

MARY WARREN: They had Doctor Griggs examine her, and she's full to the brim. And smokin' a pipe all these years, and no husband either! But she's safe, thank God, for they'll not hurt the innocent child. But be that not a marvel? You must see it, sir, it's God's work we do. So I'll be gone every day for some time. I'm – I am

1 **upright**: (here) honest and respectable 2 **recite sth.**: say sth. that you have learned 7 **strained**: not relaxed 12 **instant**: second 23–24 **full to the brim**: completely full (here: very pregnant)

an official of the court, they say, and I – [*She has been edging toward offstage.*]

PROCTOR: I'll official you! [*He strides to the mantel, takes down the whip hanging there.*]

MARY WARREN [*terrified, but coming erect, striving for her authority*]: I'll not stand whipping any more!

ELIZABETH [*hurriedly, as* PROCTOR *approaches*]: Mary, promise now you'll stay at home –

MARY WARREN [*backing from him, but keeping her erect posture, striving, striving for her way*]: The Devil's loose in Salem, Mr Proctor; we must discover where he's hiding!

PROCTOR: I'll whip the Devil out of you! [*With whip raised he reaches out for her, and she streaks away and yells.*]

MARY WARREN [*pointing at* ELIZABETH]: I saved her life today! [*Silence. His whip comes down.*]

ELIZABETH [*softly*]: I am accused?

MARY WARREN [*quaking*]: Somewhat mentioned. But I said I never see no sign you ever sent your spirit out to hurt no one, and seeing I do live so closely with you, they dismissed it.

ELIZABETH: Who accused me?

MARY WARREN: I am bound by law, I cannot tell it. [*To* PROCTOR]: I only hope you'll not be so sarcastical no more. Four judges and the King's deputy sat to dinner with us but an hour ago. I – I would have you speak civilly to me, from this out.

1 **edge** (v): move slowly 3 **I'll official you!** (infml): I'll beat you **stride**: walk with long steps **mantel**: short for mantelpiece: a shelf above a fireplace 5 **erect**: (here) standing straight **stand sth.**: tolerate sth. 9 **posture** ['pɒstʃə(r)]: the way you hold your body 13 **streak**: (here) move very fast 19 **dismiss sth.**: stop talking about sth. in court 22 **sarcastical**: (here) showing lack of respect for sb. 23 **but** (old use): only 24 **civilly**: politely **from this out** (old-fashioned): from now on

PROCTOR [*in horror, muttering in disgust at her*]: Go to bed.

MARY WARREN [*with a stamp of her foot*]: I'll not be ordered to bed no more, Mr Proctor! I am eighteen and a woman, however single!

PROCTOR: Do you wish to sit up? Then sit up.

MARY WARREN: I wish to go to bed!

PROCTOR [*in anger*]: Good night, then!

MARY WARREN: Good night. [*Dissatisfied, uncertain of herself, she goes out. Wide-eyed, both,* PROCTOR *and* ELIZABETH *stand staring.*]

ELIZABETH [*quietly*]: Oh, the noose, the noose is up!

PROCTOR: There'll be no noose.

ELIZABETH: She wants me dead. I knew all week it would come to this!

PROCTOR [*without conviction*]: They dismissed it. You heard her say –

ELIZABETH: And what of tomorrow? She will cry me out until they take me!

PROCTOR: Sit you down.

ELIZABETH: She wants me dead, John, you know it!

PROCTOR: I say sit down! [*She sits, trembling. He speaks quietly, trying to keep his wits.*] Now we must be wise, Elizabeth.

ELIZABETH [*with sarcasm, and a sense of being lost*]: Oh, indeed, indeed!

PROCTOR: Fear nothing. I'll find Ezekiel Cheever. I'll tell him she said it were all sport.

5 **sit up** (old-fashioned): not go to bed yet 8 **dissatisfied**: not happy with
10 **noose**: rope tied in a circle, used to hang a person 14 **conviction**: certainty
16 **cry sb. out**: (here) accuse sb. 22 **sense**: feeling

ELIZABETH: John, with so many in the jail, more than Cheever's help is needed now, I think. Would you favour me with this? Go to Abigail.

PROCTOR [*his soul hardening as he senses …*]: What have I to say to Abigail?

ELIZABETH [*delicately*]: John – grant me this. You have a faulty understanding of young girls. There is a promise made in any bed –

PROCTOR [*striving against his anger*]: What promise?

ELIZABETH: Spoke or silent, a promise is surely made. And she may dote on it now – I am sure she does – and thinks to kill me, then to take my place.
[*Proctor's anger is tiring; he cannot speak.*]

ELIZABETH: It is her dearest hope, John, I know it. There be a thousand names; why does she call mine? There be a certain danger in calling such a name – I am no Goody Good that sleeps in ditches, nor Osburn, drunk and half-witted. She'd dare not call out such a farmer's wife but there be monstrous profit in it. She thinks to take my place, John.

PROCTOR: She cannot think it! [*He knows it is true.*]

ELIZABETH [*reasonably*]: John, have you ever shown her somewhat of contempt? She cannot pass you in the church but you will blush –

PROCTOR: I may blush for my sin.

ELIZABETH: I think she sees another meaning in that blush.

PROCTOR: And what see you? What see you, Elizabeth?

6 **delicately** ['delɪkətli]: carefully 10 **spoke** (old use): spoken 11 **dote on sth.**: love sth. very much 17 **half-witted** (derog.): very stupid 18 **but there be** (old-fashioned): if there were not **monstrous**: (here) very large 21 **reasonably** (adv): *vernünftig* 22 **contempt**: lack of respect

ELIZABETH [*conceding*]: I think you be somewhat ashamed, for I am there, and she so close.

PROCTOR: When will you know me, woman? Were I stone I would have cracked for shame this seven month!

ELIZABETH: Then go and tell her she's a whore. Whatever promise she may sense – break it, John, break it.

PROCTOR [*between his teeth*]: Good, then. I'll go. [*He starts for his rifle.*]

ELIZABETH [*trembling, fearfully*]: Oh, how unwillingly!

PROCTOR [*turning on her, rifle in hand*]: I will curse her hotter than the oldest cinder in hell. But pray, begrudge me not my anger!

ELIZABETH: Your anger! I only ask you –

PROCTOR: Woman, am I so base? Do you truly think me base?

ELIZABETH: I never called you base.

PROCTOR: Then how do you charge me with such a promise? The promise that a stallion gives a mare I gave that girl!

ELIZABETH: Then why do you anger with me when I bid you break it?

PROCTOR: Because it speaks deceit, and I am honest! But I'll plead no more! I see now your spirit twists around the single error of my life, and I will never tear it free!

ELIZABETH [*crying out*]: You'll tear it free – when you come to know that I will be your only wife, or no wife at all! She has an arrow in you yet, John Proctor, and you know it well!

1 **concede [kən'siːd]**: admit that the other person is right 8 **rifle**: long gun
10 **curse sb.**: say rude things to sb. 11 **cinder**: piece of wood or coal that is burnt on a fire 14 **base** (adj): with no moral principles 16 **mare**: female horse
19 **deceit**: dishonest behaviour 20 **twist around sth.**: (here) hold on to sth. very tightly 23 **arrow**: *Pfeil*

[Quite suddenly, as though from the air, a figure appears in the doorway. They start slightly. It is MR HALE. *He is different now – drawn a little, and there is a quality of deference, even of guilt, about his manner now.]*

HALE: Good evening.

PROCTOR [*still in his shock*]: Why, Mr Hale! Good evening to you, sir. Come in, come in.

HALE [*to* ELIZABETH]: I hope I do not startle you.

ELIZABETH: No, no, it's only that I heard no horse –

HALE: You are Goodwife Proctor.

PROCTOR: Aye; Elizabeth.

HALE [*nods, then*]: I hope you're not off to bed yet.

PROCTOR [*setting down his gun*]: No, no. [HALE *comes farther into the room. And* PROCTOR, *to explain his nervousness*]: We are not used to visitors after dark, but you're welcome here. Will you sit you down, sir?

HALE: I will. [*He sits.*] Let you sit, Goodwife Proctor.
[*She does, never letting him out of her sight. There is a pause as* HALE *looks about the room.*]

PROCTOR [*to break the silence*]: Will you drink cider, Mr Hale?

HALE: No, it rebels my stomach; I have some further travelling yet tonight. Sit you down, sir. [PROCTOR *sits.*] I will not keep you long, but I have some business with you.

PROCTOR: Business of the court?

2 **start** (v): react out of shock 3 **drawn** (adj): looking pale because of tiredness or worry 8 **startle sb.**: give sb. a shock by surprising them 10 **Goodwife** (old-fashioned): polite form of address for a married woman 21 **rebel your stomach** (old use) **[rɪˈbel]**: make you feel sick

HALE: No – no, I come of my own, without the court's authority. Hear me. [*He wets his lips.*] I know not if you are aware, but your wife's name is – mentioned in the court.

PROCTOR: We know it, sir. Our Mary Warren told us. We are entirely amazed.

HALE: I am a stranger here, as you know. And in my ignorance I find it hard to draw a clear opinion of them that come accused before the court. And so this afternoon, and now tonight, I go from house to house – I come now from Rebecca Nurse's house and –

ELIZABETH [*shocked*]: Rebecca's charged!

HALE: God forbid such a one be charged. She is, however – mentioned somewhat.

ELIZABETH [*with an attempt at a laugh*]: You will never believe, I hope, that Rebecca trafficked with the Devil.

HALE: Woman, it is possible.

PROCTOR [*taken aback*]: Surely you cannot think so.

HALE: This is a strange time, Mister. No man may longer doubt the powers of the dark are gathered in monstrous attack upon this village. There is too much evidence now to deny it. You will agree, sir?

PROCTOR [*evading*]: I – have no knowledge in that line. But it's hard to think so pious a woman be secretly a Devil's bitch after seventy year of such good prayer.

HALE: Aye. But the Devil is a wily one, you cannot deny it. However, she is far from accused, and I know she will not be. [*Pause.*] I thought, sir, to put some questions as to the Christian characters of this house, if you'll permit me.

1 **of my own**: because I want to **authority**: (here) *Befugnis* 5 **amazed**: very surprised 16 **taken aback**: shocked 21 **evade**: not talk about sth. directly 22 **pious**: very religious **the Devil's bitch** (derog.): a woman who has a (possibly sexual) relationship with the devil 26 **as to**: about

PROCTOR [*coldly, resentful*]: Why, we – have no fear of questions, sir.

HALE: Good, then. [*He makes himself more comfortable.*] In the book of record that Mr Parris keeps, I note that you are rarely in the church on Sabbath Day.

PROCTOR: No, sir, you are mistaken.

HALE: Twenty-six time in seventeen month, sir. I must call that rare. Will you tell me why you are so absent?

PROCTOR: Mr Hale, I never knew I must account to that man for I come to church or stay at home. My wife were sick this winter.

HALE: So I am told. But you, Mister, why could you not come alone?

PROCTOR: I surely did come when I could, and when I could not I prayed in this house.

HALE: Mr Proctor, your house is not a church; your theology must tell you that.

PROCTOR: It does, sir, it does; and it tells me that a minister may pray to God without he have golden candlesticks upon the altar.

HALE: What golden candlesticks?

PROCTOR: Since we built the church there were pewter candlesticks upon the altar; Francis Nurse made them, y'know, and a sweeter hand never touched the metal. But Parris came, and for twenty week he preach nothin' but golden candlesticks until he had them. I labour the earth from dawn of day to blink of night, and I tell you true, when I look to heaven and see my money glaring at his elbows – it hurt my prayer, sir, it hurt my prayer. I think, sometimes, the man dreams cathedrals, not clapboard meetin' houses.

1 **resentful**: feeling angry 3 **book of record**: (here) register of people who attend religious meetings 7 **absent**: not present 16 **candlestick**: object that holds a candle 18 **pewter**: *Zinn* 22 **labour** (v): work hard **blink of night**: the beginning of night 23 **glare** (v): shine brightly 25 **clapboard**: thin wooden boards that cover the sides of a house

HALE [*thinks, then*]: And yet, Mister, a Christian on Sabbath Day must be in church. [*Pause.*] Tell me – you have three children?

PROCTOR: Aye. Boys.

HALE: How comes it that only two are baptized?

PROCTOR [*starts to speak, then stops, then, as though unable to restrain this*]: I like it not that Mr Parris should lay his hand upon my baby. I see no light of God in that man. I'll not conceal it.

HALE: I must say it, Mr Proctor; that is not for you to decide. The man's ordained, therefore the light of God is in him.

PROCTOR [*flushed with resentment but trying to smile*]: What's your suspicion, Mr Hale?

HALE: No, no, I have no –

PROCTOR: I nailed the roof upon the church, I hung the door –

HALE: Oh, did you! That's a good sign, then.

PROCTOR: It may be I have been too quick to bring the man to book, but you cannot think we ever desired the destruction of religion. I think that's in your mind, is it not?

HALE [*not altogether giving way*]: I – have – there is a softness in your record, sir, a softness.

ELIZABETH: I think, maybe, we have been too hard with Mr Parris. I think so. But sure we never loved the Devil here.

HALE [*nods, deliberating this. Then, with the voice of one administering a secret test*]: Do you know your Commandments, Elizabeth?

5 **restrain sth**: hold sth. back 7 **conceal**: (here) deny 9 **ordain sb.**: officially make sb. a priest 10 **flushed**: red in the face 15–16 **bring sb. to book**: judge and punish sb. 18 **give way**: give up your argument **softness** (old use): (here) problem, weakness of character 22 **deliberate sth.**: think carefully about sth. **administer sth.**: carry sth. out

ELIZABETH [*without hesitation, even eagerly*]: I surely do. There be no mark of blame upon my life, Mr Hale. I am a covenanted Christian woman.

HALE: And you, Mister?

PROCTOR [*a trifle unsteadily*]: I – am sure I do, sir.

HALE [*glances at her open face, then at* JOHN, *then*]: Let you repeat them, if you will.

PROCTOR: The Commandments.

HALE: Aye.

PROCTOR [*looking off, beginning to sweat*]: Thou shalt not kill.

HALE: Aye.

PROCTOR [*counting on his fingers*]: Thou shalt not steal. Thou shalt not covet thy neighbour's goods, nor make unto thee any graven image. Thou shalt not take the name of the Lord in vain; thou shalt have no other gods before me. [*With some hesitation*] Thou shalt remember the Sabbath Day and keep it holy. [*Pause. Then*] Thou shalt honour thy father and mother. Thou shalt not bear false witness. [*He is stuck. He counts back on his fingers, knowing one if missing.*] Thou shalt not make unto thee any graven image.

HALE: You have said that twice, sir.

PROCTOR [*lost*]: Aye. [*He is flailing for it.*]

ELIZABETH [*delicately*]: Adultery, John.

1 **hesitation**: waiting slightly 2 **covenanted**: (here) being a member of a church and sticking to its laws 5 **a trifle**: a little bit 10 **thou shalt** (old-fashioned): you shall (used in the bible to introduce each of the Ten Commandments) 13 **covet sth.**: want sth. very much **thy** (old use): your **make unto thee** (old use): make for yourself 13–14 **graven image**: sculpture that represents a particular person or thing 14 **take sb.'s name in vain**: use sb.'s name in a disrespectful manner 17–18 **bear false witness**: tell lies about people 18 **be stuck**: not know how to continue 21 **flail for sth.**: (here) search for sth. very hard 22 **adultery**: when a married person has sex with sb. who is not their husband or wife

PROCTOR [*as though a secret arrow had pained his heart*]: Aye. [*Trying to grin it away – to* HALE] You see, sir, between the two of us we do know them all. [HALE *only looks at* PROCTOR, *deep in his attempt to define this man.* PROCTOR *grows more uneasy.*] I think it be a small fault.

HALE: Theology, sir, is a fortress; no crack in a fortress may be accounted small. [*He rises; he seems worried now. He paces a little, in deep thought.*]

PROCTOR: There be no love for Satan in this house, Mister.

HALE: I pray it, I pray it dearly. [*He looks to both of them, an attempt at a smile on his face, but his misgivings are clear.*] Well, then – I'll bid you good night.

ELIZABETH [*unable to restrain herself*]: Mr Hale.
[*He turns.*]
I do think you are suspecting me somewhat? Are you not?

HALE [*obviously disturbed – and evasive*]: Goody Proctor, I do not judge you. My duty is to add what I may to the godly wisdom of the court. I pray you both good health and good fortune. [*To* JOHN] Good night, sir. [*He starts out.*]

ELIZABETH [*with a note of desperation*]: I think you must tell him, John.

HALE: What's that?

ELIZABETH [*restraining a call*]: Will you tell him?
[*Slight pause.* HALE *looks questioningly at* JOHN.]

2 **awe**: great respect 4 **uneasy**: feeling worried 6 **fortress**: a very strong building built for defense against an attack 7 **pace** (v): walk up and down worriedly
11 **misgiving**: worry 13 **restrain yourself**: stop yourself from doing sth.
16 **disturbed**: unhappy **evasive**: not wanting to say sth. openly 18 **pray sb. sth.** (old use): pray that God give sth. to sb. 20 **desperation**: (here) great worry

PROCTOR [*with difficulty*]: I – I have no witness and cannot prove it, except my word be taken. But I know the children's sickness had naught to do with witchcraft.

HALE [*stopped, struck*]: Naught to do – ?

PROCTOR: Mr Parris discovered them sportin' in the woods. They were startled and took sick.
[*Pause.*]

HALE: Who told you this?

PROCTOR [*hesitates, then*]: Abigail Williams.

HALE: Abigail!

PROCTOR: Aye.

HALE [*his eyes wide*]: Abigail Williams told you it had naught to do with witchcraft!

PROCTOR: She told me the day you came, sir.

HALE [*suspiciously*]: Why – why did you keep this?

PROCTOR: I never knew until tonight that the world is gone daft with this nonsense.

HALE: Nonsense! Mister, I have myself examined Tituba, Sarah Good, and numerous others that have confessed to dealing with the Devil. They have *confessed* it.

PROCTOR: And why not, if they must hang for denyin' it? There are them that will swear to anything before they'll hang; have you never thought of that?

HALE: I have. I – I have indeed. [*It is his own suspicion, but he resists it. He glances at* ELIZABETH, *then at* JOHN.] And you – would you testify to this in court?

5 **sport** (v, old-fashioned): run around playfully 16–17 **go daft with sth.**: go crazy because of sth.

PROCTOR: I – had not reckoned with goin' into court. But if I must I will.

HALE: Do you falter here?

PROCTOR: I falter nothing, but I may wonder if my story will be credited in such a court. I do wonder on it, when such a steady-minded minister as you will suspicion such a woman that never lied, and cannot, and the world knows she cannot! I may falter somewhat, Mister; I am no fool.

HALE [*quietly – it has impressed him*]: Proctor, let you open with me now, for I have a rumour that troubles me. It's said you hold no belief that there may even be witches in the world. Is that true, sir?

PROCTOR [*he knows this is critical, and is striving against his disgust with* HALE *and with himself for even answering*]: I know not what I have said, I may have said it. I have wondered if there be witches in the world – although I cannot believe they come among us now.

HALE: Then you do not believe –

PROCTOR: I have no knowledge of it; the Bible speaks of witches, and I will not deny them.

HALE: And you, woman?

ELIZABETH: I – I cannot believe it.

HALE [*shocked*]: You cannot!

PROCTOR: Elizabeth, you bewilder him!

ELIZABETH [*to* HALE]: I cannot think the Devil may own a woman's soul, Mr Hale, when she keeps an upright way, as I have. I am a good woman, I know it; and if you believe I may do only good

5 **credit sth.**: believe sth. 5–6 **steady-minded**: sensible 9 **let you open with me** (old use): tell me the truth 13–14 **disgust with sb.**: strong dislike for sb. 24 **bewilder sb.**: confuse sb.

work in the world, and yet be secretly bound to Satan, then I must tell you, sir, I do not believe it.

HALE: But, woman, you do believe there are witches in –

ELIZABETH: If you think that I am one, then I say there are none.

HALE: You surely do not fly against the Gospel, the Gospel –

PROCTOR: She believe in the Gospel, every word!

ELIZABETH: Question Abigail Williams about the Gospel, not myself!
[HALE *stares at her*.]

PROCTOR: She do not mean to doubt the Gospel, sir, you cannot think it. This be a Christian house, sir, a Christian house.

HALE: God keep you both; let the third child be quickly baptized, and go you without fail each Sunday in to Sabbath prayer; and keep a solemn, quiet way among you. I think – [GILES COREY *appears in doorway*.]

GILES: John!

PROCTOR: Giles! What's the matter?

GILES: They take my wife.
[FRANCIS NURSE *enters*.]

GILES: And his Rebecca!

PROCTOR [*to* FRANCIS]: Rebecca's in the *jail*!

FRANCIS: Aye, Cheever come and take her in his wagon. We've only now come from the jail, and they'll not even let us to see them.

ELIZABETH: They've surely gone wild now, Mr Hale!

FRANCIS [*going to* HALE]: Reverend Hale! Can you not speak to the Deputy Governor? I'm sure he mistakes these people –

5 **fly against sth.**: turn against sth. 13 **without fail**: with no exceptions

HALE: Pray calm yourself, Mr Nurse.

FRANCIS: My wife is the very brick and mortar of the church, Mr Hale – [*indicating* GILES] – and Martha Corey, there cannot be a woman closer yet to God than Martha.

HALE: How is Rebecca charged, Mr Nurse?

FRANCIS [*with a mocking, half-hearted laugh*]: For murder, she's charged! [*Mockingly quoting the warrant*] 'For the marvellous and supernatural murder of Goody Putnam's babies.' What am I to do, Mr Hale?

HALE [*turns from* FRANCIS, *deeply troubled, then*]: Believe me, Mr Nurse, if Rebecca Nurse be tainted, then nothing's left to stop the whole green world from burning. Let you rest upon the justice of the court; the court will send her home, I know it.

FRANCIS: You cannot mean she will be tried in court!

HALE [*pleading*]: Nurse, though our hearts break, we cannot flinch; these are new times, sir. There is a misty plot afoot so subtle we should be criminal to cling to old respects and ancient friendships. I have seen too many frightful proofs in court – the Devil is alive in Salem, and we dare not quail to follow wherever the accusing finger points!

PROCTOR [*angered*]: How may such a woman murder children?

HALE [*in great pain*]: Man, remember, until an hour before the Devil fell, God thought him beautiful in Heaven.

GILES: I never said my wife were a witch, Mr Hale; I only said she were reading books!

2 **mortar**: grey mixture used in building to make the bricks stick together (brick and mortar (fig.): person who holds the church community together) 7 **warrant**: official document that allows you to do sth. (e.g. arrest sb.) 11 **tainted**: with signs of being morally wrong 15 **flinch**: instinctively move away from sth. unpleasant 16 **misty**: unable to be seen clearly **subtle** ['sʌtl]: not easily noticed 19 **quail to do sth.**: (here) be afraid to do sth.

HALE: Mr Corey, exactly what complaint were made on your wife?

GILES: That bloody mongrel Walcott charge her. Y'see, he buy a pig of my wife four or five year ago, and the pig died soon after. So he come dancin' in for his money back. So my Martha, she says to him, 'Walcott, if you haven't the wit to feed a pig properly, you'll not live to own many,' she says. Now he goes to court and claims that from that day to this he cannot keep a pig alive for more than four weeks because my Martha bewitch them with her books! [*Enter* EZEKIEL CHEEVER. *A shocked silence.*]

CHEEVER: Good evening to you, Proctor.

PROCTOR: Why, Mr Cheever. Good evening.

CHEEVER: Good evening, all. Good evening, Mr Hale.

PROCTOR: I hope you come not on business of the court.

CHEEVER: I do, Proctor, aye. I am clerk of the court now, y'know. [*Enter* MARSHAL HERRICK, *a man is his early thirties, who is somewhat shamefaced at the moment.*]

GILES: It's a pity, Ezekiel, that an honest tailor might have gone to Heaven must burn in Hell. You'll burn for this, do you know it?

CHEEVER: You know yourself I must do as I'm told. You surely know that, Giles. And I'd as lief you'd not be sending me to Hell. I like not the sound of it, I tell you; I like not the sound of it. [*He fears* PROCTOR, *but starts to reach inside his coat.*] Now believe me, Proctor, how heavy be the law, all its tonnage I do carry on my back tonight. [*He takes out a warrant.*] I have a warrant for your wife.

PROCTOR [*to* HALE]: You said she were not charged!

HALE: I know nothin' of it. [*To* CHEEVER] When were she charged?

2 **mongrel** (derog.): dog of mixed breed (term used to show disrespect to people) 16 **shamefaced**: embarrassed 20 **I'd as lief** (old use): I would prefer 23 **tonnage** ['tʌnɪdʒ]: weight

CHEEVER: I am given sixteen warrant tonight, sir, and she is one.

PROCTOR: Who charged her?

CHEEVER: Why, Abigail Williams charge her.

PROCTOR: On what proof, what proof?

CHEEVER [*looking about the room*]: Mr Proctor, I have little time. The court bid me search your house, but I like not to search a house. So will you hand me any poppets that your wife may keep here?

PROCTOR: Poppets?

ELIZABETH: I have kept no poppets, not since I were a girl.

CHEEVER [*embarrassed, glancing toward the mantel where sits* MARY WARREN'S *poppet*]: I spy a poppet, Goody Proctor.

ELIZABETH: Oh! [*Going for it*]: Why, this is Mary's.

CHEEVER [*shyly*]: Would you please to give it to me?

ELIZABETH [*handing it to him, asks* HALE]: Has the court discovered a text in poppets now?

CHEEVER [*carefully holding the poppet*]: Do you keep any others in this house?

PROCTOR: No, nor this one either till tonight. What signifies a poppet?

CHEEVER: Why, a poppet – [*he gingerly turns the poppet over*] – a poppet may signify – Now, woman, will you please to come with me?

PROCTOR: She will not! [*To* ELIZABETH] Fetch Mary here.

CHEEVER [*ineptly reaching toward* ELIZABETH]: No, no, I am forbid to leave her from my sight.

11 **spy sth.**: see sth. 20 **gingerly**: carefully 24 **ineptly**: not effectively

PROCTOR [*pushing his arm away*]: You'll leave her out of sight and out of mind, Mister. Fetch Mary, Elizabeth.
[ELIZABETH *goes upstairs.*]

HALE: What signifies a poppet, Mr Cheever?

CHEEVER [*turning the poppet over in his hands*]: Why, they say it may signify that she – [*He has lifted the poppet's skirt, and his eyes widen in astonished fear.*] Why, this, this –

PROCTOR [*reaching for the poppet*]: What's there?

CHEEVER: Why – [*He draws out a long needle from the poppet*] it is a needle! Herrick, Herrick, it is a needle!
[HERRICK *comes toward him.*]

PROCTOR [*angrily, bewildered*]: And what signifies a needle!

CHEEVER [*his hands shaking*]: Why, this go hard with her, Proctor, this – I had my doubts, Proctor, I had my doubts, but here's calamity. [*To* HALE, *showing the needle*] You see it, sir, it is a needle!

HALE: Why? What meanin' has it?

CHEEVER [*wide-eyed, trembling*]: The girl, the Williams girl, Abigail Williams, sir. She sat to dinner in Reverend Parris's house tonight, and without word nor warnin' she falls to the floor. Like a struck beast, he says, and screamed a scream that a bull would weep to hear. And he goes to save her, and, stuck two inches in the flesh of her belly, he draw a needle out. And demandin' of her how she come to be so stabbed, she – [*to* PROCTOR *now*] – testify it were your wife's familiar spirit pushed it in.

PROCTOR: Why, she done it herself! [*To* HALE] I hope you're not takin' this for proof, Mister!
[HALE, *struck by the proof, is silent.*]

9 **needle**: *Nagel* 13 **this go hard with you** (old use): this will be a big problem for you 15 **calamity**: disaster 19–20 **struck beast**: wild animal that has been hit by a spear 23 **stab sb.**: hurt sb. by sticking a sharp object into them

CHEEVER: 'Tis hard proof! [*To* HALE] I find here a poppet Goody Proctor keeps. I have found it, sir. And in the belly of the poppet a needle's stuck. I tell you true, Proctor, I never warranted to see such proof of Hell, and I bid you obstruct me not, for I –

[*Enter* ELIZABETH *with* MARY WARREN. PROCTOR, *seeing* MARY WARREN, *draws her by the arm to* HALE.]

PROCTOR: Here now! Mary, how did this poppet come into my house?

MARY WARREN [*frightened for herself, her voice very small*]: What poppet's that, sir?

PROCTOR [*impatiently, pointing at the doll in* CHEEVER'S *hand*]: This poppet, this poppet.

MARY WARREN [*evasively, looking at it*]: Why, I – I think it is mine.

PROCTOR: It is your poppet, is it not?

MARY WARREN [*not understanding the direction of this*]: It – is, sir.

PROCTOR: And how did it come into this house?

MARY WARREN [*glancing about at the avid faces*]: Why – I made it in the court, sir, and – give it to Goody Proctor tonight.

PROCTOR [*to* HALE]: Now, sir – do you have it?

HALE: Mary Warren, a needle have been found inside this poppet.

MARY WARREN [*bewildered*]: Why, I meant no harm by it, sir.

PROCTOR [*quickly*]: You stuck that needle in yourself?

MARY WARREN: I – I believe I did, sir, I –

PROCTOR [*to* HALE]: What say you now?

HALE [*watching* MARY WARREN *closely*]: Child, you are certain this be your natural memory? May it be, perhaps, that someone conjures you even now to say this?

3 **warrant** (v, old-fashioned): think 4 **obstruct sb.**: stop sb.

MARY WARREN: Conjures me? Why, no, sir, I am entirely myself, I think. Let you ask Susanna Walcott – she saw me sewin' it in court. [*Or better still*] Ask Abby, Abby sat beside me when I made it.

PROCTOR [*to* HALE, *of* CHEEVER]: Bid him begone. Your mind is surely settled now. Bid him out, Mr Hale.

ELIZABETH: What signifies a needle?

HALE: Mary – you charge a cold and cruel murder on Abigail.

MARY WARREN: Murder! I charge no –

HALE: Abigail were stabbed tonight; a needle were found stuck into her belly –

ELIZABETH: And she charges me?

HALE: Aye.

ELIZABETH [*her breath knocked out*]: Why – ! The girl is murder! She must be ripped out of the world!

CHEEVER [*pointing at* ELIZABETH]: You've heard that, sir! Ripped out of the world! Herrick, you heard it!

PROCTOR [*suddenly snatching the warrant out of* CHEEVER'S *hands*]: Out with you.

CHEEVER: Proctor, you dare not touch the warrant.

PROCTOR [*ripping the warrant*]: Out with you!

CHEEVER: You've ripped the Deputy Governor's warrant, man!

PROCTOR: Damn the Deputy Governor! Out of my house!

HALE: Now, Proctor, Proctor!

PROCTOR: Get y'gone with them! You are a broken minister.

5 **Bid him begone**: tell him to go away 18 **snatch sth.**: take sth. quickly 25 **Get y'gone!** (old-fashioned): Go away! **broken**: (here) ruined; corrupt

HALE: Proctor, if she is innocent, the court –

PROCTOR: If *she* is innocent! Why do you never wonder if Parris be innocent, or Abigail? Is the accuser always holy now? Were they born this morning as clean as God's fingers? I'll tell you what's walking Salem – vengeance is walking Salem. We are what we always were in Salem, but now the little crazy children are jangling the keys of the kingdom, and common vengeance writes the law! This warrant's vengeance! I'll not give my wife to vengeance!

ELIZABETH: I'll go, John –

PROCTOR: You will not go!

HERRICK: I have nine men outside. You cannot keep her. The law binds me, John, I cannot budge.

PROCTOR [*to* HALE, *ready to break him*]: Will you see her taken?

HALE: Proctor, the court is just –

PROCTOR: Pontius Pilate! God will not let you wash your hands of this!

ELIZABETH: John – I think I must go with them.
[*He cannot bear to look at her.*]
Mary, there is bread enough for the morning; you will bake in the afternoon. Help Mr Proctor as you were his daughter – you owe me that, and much more. [*She is fighting her weeping. To* PROCTOR] When the children wake, speak nothing of witchcraft – it will frighten them. [*She cannot go on.*]

PROCTOR: I will bring you home. I will bring you soon.

ELIZABETH: Oh, John, bring me soon!

5 **walk (a place)**: (here) visit a place in a supernatural way 7 **jangle the keys of the kingdom** (fig.): be in charge of a place 13 **budge**: (here) change one's opinion 16–17 **wash one's hands of sth.**: claim that one is not responsible for sth. (referring to **Pontius Pilate** (16) washing his hands after condemning Jesus to death)

PROCTOR: I will fall like an ocean on that court! Fear nothing, Elizabeth.

ELIZABETH [*with great fear*]: I will fear nothing. [*She looks about the room, as though to fix it in her mind.*] Tell the children I have gone to visit someone sick.
[*She walks out the door,* HERRICK *and* CHEEVER *behind her. For a moment,* PROCTOR *watches from the doorway. The clank of chain is heard.*]

PROCTOR: Herrick! Herrick, don't chain her! [*He rushes out the door. From outside*] Damn you, man, you will not chain her! Off with them! I'll not have it! I will not have her chained!
[*There are other men's voices against his.* HALE, *in a fever of guilt and uncertainty, turns from the door to avoid the sight;* MARY WARREN *bursts into tears and sits weeping.* GILES COREY *calls to* HALE.]

GILES: And yet silent, minister? It is fraud, you know it is fraud! What keeps you, man?
[PROCTOR *is half braced, half pushed into the room by two deputies and* HERRICK.]

PROCTOR: I'll pay you, Herrick, I will surely pay you!

HERRICK [*panting*]: In God's name, John, I cannot help myself. I must chain them all. Now let you keep inside this house till I am gone! [*He goes out with his deputies.*]
[PROCTOR *stands there, gulping air. Horses and a wagon creaking are beard.*]

HALE [*in great uncertainty*]: Mr Proctor –

PROCTOR: Out of my sight!

HALE: Charity, Proctor, charity. What I have heard in her favour, I will not fear to testify in court. God help me, I cannot judge her

7 **clank**: sound made by two pieces of metal hitting each other 17 **brace sb.**: support sb. 23 **gulp air**: breathe deeply **creak**: *knarren* 27 **charity**: (here) be kind **in sb.'s favour**: helping or supporting sb.

guilty or innocent – I know not. Only this consider: the world goes mad, and it profit nothing you should lay the cause to the vengeance of a little girl.

PROCTOR: You are a coward! Though you be ordained in God's own tears, you are a coward now!

HALE: Proctor, I cannot think God be provoked so grandly by such a petty cause. The jails are packed – our greatest judges sit in Salem now – and hangin's promised. Man, we must look to cause proportionate. Were there murder done, perhaps, and never brought to light? Abomination! Some secret blasphemy that stinks to Heaven? Think on cause, man, and let you help me to discover it. For there's your way, believe it, there is your only way, when such confusion strikes upon the world. [*He goes to* GILES *and* FRANCIS.] Let you counsel among yourselves; think on your village and what may have drawn from heaven such thundering wrath upon you all. I shall pray God open up our eyes.
[HALE *goes out*.]

FRANCIS [*struck by* HALE'S *mood*]: I never heard no murder done in Salem.

PROCTOR [*he has been reached by* HALE'S words]: Leave me, Francis, leave me.

GILES [*shaken*]: John – tell me, are we lost?

PROCTOR: Go home now, Giles. We'll speak on it tomorrow.

GILES: Let you think on it. We'll come early, eh?

PROCTOR: Aye. Go now, Giles.

2 **it profit nothing**: (here) it does not help **lay the cause to sth.**: blame sth.
4 **coward**: sb. who is not brave 7 **petty**: not important 8 **be promised**: (here) be likely to happen 9 **proportionate [prəˈpɔːʃənət]**: (here) suitable, appropriate
10 **blasphemy**: disrespect for God 14 **counsel [ˈkaʊnsl]**: (here) talk about a problem in order to find a solution 16 **wrath [rɒθ]**: great anger 22 **shaken**: shocked and scared

GILES: Good night, then.

[GILES COREY *goes out. After a moment*]:

MARY WARREN [*in a fearful squeak of a voice*]: Mr Proctor, very likely they'll let her come home once they're given proper evidence.

PROCTOR: You're coming to the court with me, Mary. You will tell it in the court.

MARY WARREN: I cannot charge murder on Abigail.

PROCTOR [*moving menacingly toward her*]: You will tell the court how that poppet come here and who stuck the needle in.

MARY WARREN: She'll kill me for sayin' that! [PROCTOR *continues toward her.*] Abby'll charge lechery on you, Mr Proctor!

PROCTOR [*halting*]: She's told you!

MARY WARREN: I have known it, sir. She'll ruin you with it, I know she will.

PROCTOR [*hesitating, and with deep hatred of himself*]: Good. Then her saintliness is done with. [MARY *backs from him.*] We will slide together into our pit; you will tell the court what you know.

MARY WARREN [*in terror*]: I cannot, they'll turn on me – [PROCTOR *strides and catches her, and she is repeating, 'I cannot, I cannot!'*]

PROCTOR: My wife will never die for me! I will bring your guts into your mouth but that goodness will not die for me!

MARY WARREN [*struggling to escape him*]: I cannot do it, I cannot!

PROCTOR [*grasping her by the throat as though he would strangle her*]: Make your peace with it! Now Hell and Heaven grapple on our backs, and all our old pretence is ripped away – make your

3 **squeak**: short, high sound   11 **lechery** (old-fashioned): *Unzuchtigkeit*
16 **saintliness**: holiness; goodness   **back from sb.** (v): move backwards away from sb.   17 **pit**: deep hole; (here) hell; a situation that is very bad for you   18 **turn on sb.**: attack sb., work against sb.   20–21 **bring sb.'s guts into their mouth**: force sb. to speak   24 **grapple**: fight

peace! [*He throws her to the floor, where she sobs, 'I cannot, I cannot …' And now, half to himself, staring, and turning to the open door*] Peace. It is a providence, and no great change; we are only what we always were, but naked now. [*He walks as though toward a great horror, facing the open sky*.] Aye, naked! And the wind, God's icy wind, will blow!

And she is over and over again sobbing, 'I cannot, I cannot, I cannot', as

THE CURTAIN FALLS

ACT THREE

The vestry room of the Salem meeting house, now serving as the anteroom of the General Court.

As the curtain rises, the room is empty, but for sunlight pouring through two high windows in the back wall. The room is solemn, even forbidding. Heavy beams jut out, boards of random widths make up the walls. At the right are two doors leading into the meeting house proper, where the court is being held. At the left another door leads outside.

There is a plain bench at the left, and another at the right. In the centre a rather long meeting table, with stools and a considerable armchair snugged up to it.

Through the partitioning wall at the right we hear a prosecutor's voice, JUDGE HATHORNE'S, *asking a question; then a woman's voice,* MARTHA COREY'S, *replying.*

HATHORNE'S VOICE: Now, Martha Corey, there is abundant evidence in our hands to show that you have given yourself to the reading of fortunes. Do you deny it?

MARTHA COREY'S VOICE: I am innocent to a witch. I know not what a witch is.

HATHORNE'S VOICE: How do you know, then, that you are not a witch?

MARTHA COREY'S VOICE: If I were, I would know it.

1 **vestry room**: room in a church where equipment for the service are kept and where the priest prepares for the service **anteroom** ['æntiru:m]: room in an official building where people wait before they go into a larger room 3 **but for**: except 4 **forbidding**: not inviting; threatening 5 **jut out**: stick out **random**: without a regular pattern 6 **proper**: (here) actual, real 9 **stool**: seat without a backrest **considerable**: (here) very large 10 **snugged up to it** (old use): arranged comfortably around it 11 **partitioning wall**: wall that separates one room into two parts **prosecutor**: person at court who charges sb. with a crime 14 **abundant**: much **evidence**: facts or objects used in court to show that a statement is true 15–16 **reading of fortunes**: saying what will happen in the future

HATHORNE'S VOICE: Why do you hurt these children?

MARTHA COREY'S VOICE: I do not hurt them. I scorn it!

GILES' VOICE [*roaring*]: I have evidence for the court!
[*Voices of townspeople rise in excitement.*]

DANFORTH'S VOICE: You will keep your seat!

GILES' VOICE: Thomas Putnam is reaching out for land!

DANFORTH'S VOICE: Remove that man, Marshall!

GILES' VOICE: You're hearing lies, lies!
[*A roaring goes up from the people.*]

HATHORNE'S VOICE: Arrest him, excellency!

GILES' VOICE: I have evidence. Why will you not hear my evidence?
[*The door opens and* GILES *is half carried into the vestry room by* HERRICK.]

GILES: Hands off, damn you, let me go!

HERRICK: Giles, Giles!

GILES: Out of my way, Herrick! I bring evidence –

HERRICK: You cannot go in there, Giles; it's a court!
[*Enter* HALE *from the court.*]

HALE: Pray be calm a moment.

GILES: You, Mr Hale, go in there and demand I speak.

HALE: A moment, sir, a moment.

GILES: They'll be hangin' my wife!
[JUDGE HATHORNE *enters. He is in his sixties, a bitter, remorseless Salem judge.*]

2 **scorn sth.**: not respect sth.; think very badly of sth. 10 **excellency**: form of addressing a superior official (your excellence) 23 **remorseless**: not caring about other people; cruel

HATHORNE: How do you dare come roarin' into this court! Are you gone daft, Corey?

GILES: You're not a Boston judge yet, Hathorne. You'll not call me daft!

[*Enter* DEPUTY GOVERNOR DANFORTH *and, behind him,* EZEKIEL CHEEVER *and* PARRIS. *On his appearance, silence falls.* DANFORTH *is a grave man in his sixties, of some humour and sophistication that does not, however, interfere with an exact loyalty to his position and his cause. He comes down to* GILES, *who awaits his wrath.*]

DANFORTH [*looking directly at* GILES]: Who is this man?

PARRIS: Giles Corey, sir, and a more contentious –

GILES [*to* PARRIS]: I am asked the question, and I am old enough to answer it! [*To* DANFORTH, *who impresses him and to whom he smiles through his strain.*] My name is Corey, sir, Giles Corey. I have six hundred acres, and timber in addition. It is my wife you be condemning now. [*He indicates the courtroom.*]

DANFORTH: And how do you imagine to help her cause with such contemptuous riot? Now be gone. Your old age alone keeps you out of jail for this.

GILES [*beginning to plead*]: They be tellin' lies about my wife, sir, I –

DANFORTH: Do you take it upon yourself to determine what this court shall believe and what it shall set aside?

GILES: Your Excellency, we mean no disrespect for –

DANFORTH: Disrespect indeed! It is disruption, Mister. This is the highest court of the supreme government of this province, do you know it?

7 **grave**: very serious **sophistication**: (here) with wide knowledge of the world 8 **interfere with**: (here) have an influence on 11 **contentious [kən'tenʃəs]**: frequently involved in arguments 14 **strain**: *Anspannung* 18 **contemptuous [kən'temptʃuəs]**: disrespectful **riot**: (here) disorderly behaviour 21 **take it upon oneself to do sth.**: do sth. that you have no authority to do 22 **set aside**: not consider any further 25 **supreme**: most important

GILES [*beginning to weep*]: Your Excellency, I only said she were readin' books, sir, and they come and take her out of my house for –

DANFORTH [*mystified*]: Books! What books?

GILES [*through helpless sobs*]: It is my third wife, sir; I never had no wife that be so taken with books, and I thought to find the cause of it, d'y'see, but it were no witch I blamed her for. [*He is openly weeping.*] I have broke charity with the woman, I have broke charity with her. [*He covers his face, ashamed.* DANFORTH *is respectfully silent.*]

HALE: Excellency, he claims hard evidence for his wife's defence. I think that in all justice you must –

DANFORTH: Then let him submit his evidence in proper affidavit. You are certainly aware of our procedure here, Mr Hale. [*To* HERRICK] Clear this room.

HERRICK: Come now, Giles. [*He gently pushes* COREY *out.*]

FRANCIS: We are desperate, sir; we come here three days now and cannot be heard.

DANFORTH: Who is this man?

FRANCIS: Francis Nurse, Your Excellency.

HALE: His wife's Rebecca that were condemned this morning.

DANFORTH: Indeed! I am amazed to find you in such uproar. I have only good report of your character, Mr Nurse.

HATHORNE: I think they must both be arrested in contempt, sir.

4 **mystified**: confused 8–9 **break charity with sb..**: do bad things to sb.
13 **submit sth.**: present sth. to an authority **affidavit [ˌæfəˈdeɪvɪt]**: *eidesstattliche Erklärung* 14 **procedure**: official way of organizing sth. (e.g. a court trial)
15 **clear sth.**: remove everything from sth. (e.g. a place) 22 **be in uproar**: protest very loudly against sth. 24 **arrest sb. in contempt**: arrest sb. because they disrespect the court

DANFORTH [*to* FRANCIS]: Let you write your plea, and in due time I will –

FRANCIS: Excellency, we have proof for your eyes; God forbid you shut them to it. The girls, sir, the girls are frauds.

DANFORTH: What's that?

FRANCIS: We have proof of it, sir. They are all deceiving you. [DANFORTH *is shocked, but studying* FRANCIS.]

HATHORNE: This is contempt, sir, contempt!

DANFORTH: Peace, Judge Hathorne. Do you know who I am, Mr Nurse?

FRANCIS: I surely do, sir, and I think you must be a wise judge to be what you are.

DANFORTH: And do you know that near to four hundred are in the jails from Marblehead to Lynn, and upon my signature?

FRANCIS: I –

DANFORTH: And seventy-two condemned to hang by that signature?

FRANCIS: Excellency, I never thought to say it to such a weighty judge, but you are deceived.

[*Enter* GILES COREY *from left. All turns to see as he beckons in* MARY WARREN *with* PROCTOR. MARY *is keeping her eyes to the ground;* PROCTOR *has her elbow as though she were near collapse.*]

PARRIS [*on seeing her, in shock*]: Mary Warren! [*He goes directly to bend close to her face.*] What are you about here?

PROCTOR [*pressing* PARRIS *away from her with a gentle but firm motion of protectiveness*]: She would speak with the Deputy Governor.

1 **plea**: statement made by someone in court **in due time [dju:]**: when the right time comes 6 **deceive sb. [dɪ'siːv]**: make sb. believe sth. that is not true
19 **beckon sb.** *jdn heranwinken* **21 collapse**: break down, fall over with weakness
23 **What are you about here?**: Why are you here? 25 **protectiveness**: acting in a way to keep sth. bad away from sb. **she would** (old-fashioned): she wants to

DANFORTH [*shocked by this, turns to* HERRICK]: Did you not tell me Mary Warren were sick in bed?

HERRICK: She were, Your Honour. When I go to fetch her to the court last week, she said she were sick.

GILES: She has been strivin' with her soul all week, Your Honour; she comes now to tell the truth of this to you.

DANFORTH: Who is this?

PROCTOR: John Proctor, sir. Elizabeth Proctor is my wife.

PARRIS: Beware this man, Your Excellency, this man is mischief.

HALE [*excitedly*]: I think you must hear the girl, sir, she –

DANFORTH [*who has become very interested in* MARY WARREN *and only raises a hand toward* HALE]: Peace. What would you tell us, Mary Warren?
[PROCTOR *looks at her, but she cannot speak.*]

PROCTOR: She never saw no spirits, sir.

DANFORTH [*with great alarm and surprise, to* MARY]: Never saw no spirits!

GILES [*eagerly*]: Never.

PROCTOR [*reaching into his jacket*]: She has signed a deposition, sir –

DANFORTH [*instantly*]: No, no, I accept no depositions. [*He is rapidly calculating this; he turns from her to* PROCTOR.] Tell me, Mr Proctor, have you given out this story in the village?

PROCTOR: We have not.

PARRIS: They've come to overthrow the court, sir! This man is –

5 **strive with sth.** (old use): be in conflict with sth. 9 **beware sb.**: be careful with sb. who might be dangerous 20 **deposition**: formal, written statement for use in court **instantly**: immediately, very quickly

DANFORTH: I pray you, Mr Parris. Do you know, Mr Proctor, that the entire contention of the state in these trials is that the voice of Heaven is speaking through the children?

PROCTOR: I know that, sir.

DANFORTH [*thinks, staring at* PROCTOR, *then turns to* MARY WARREN]: And you, Mary Warren, how came you to cry out people for sending their spirits against you?

MARY WARREN: It were pretence, sir.

DANFORTH: I cannot hear you.

PROCTOR: It were pretence, she says.

DANFORTH: Ah? And the other girls? Susanna Walcott, and – the others? They are also pretending?

MARY WARREN: Aye, sir.

DANFORTH [*wide-eyed*]: Indeed. [*Pause. He is baffed by this. He turns to study* PROCTOR'S *face.*]

PARRIS [*in a sweat*]: Excellency, you surely cannot think to let so vile a lie be spread in open court!

DANFORTH: Indeed not, but it strike hard upon me that she will dare come here with such a tale. Now, Mr Proctor, before I decide whether I shall hear you or not, it is my duty to tell you this. We burn a hot fire here; it melts down all concealment.

PROCTOR: I know that, sir.

DANFORTH: Let me continue. I understand well, a husband's tenderness may drive him to extravagance in defence of a wife. Are you certain in your conscience, Mister, that your evidence is the truth?

2 **contention**: (here) belief that forms the basis of a case 8 **pretence**: acting in a way that makes others believe lies 16 **vile**: morally bad 18 **strike upon sb.** (old use): be noticed by sb. suddenly 21 **concealment**: *Geheimhaltung*
23–24 **tenderness**: (here) love 24 **extravagance**: (here) extreme behaviour
25 **conscience**: ability to decide what is morally right or wrong

PROCTOR: It is. And you will surely know it.

DANFORTH: And you thought to declare this revelation in the open court before the public?

PROCTOR: I thought I would, aye - with your permission.

DANFORTH [*his eyes narrowing*]: Now, sir, what is your purpose in so doing?

PROCTOR: Why, I – I would free my wife, sir.

DANFORTH: There lurks nowhere in your heart, nor hidden in your spirit, any desire to undermine this court?

PROCTOR [*with the faintest faltering*]: Why, no, sir.

CHEEVER [*clears his throat, awakening*]: I – Your Excellency.

DANFORTH: Mr Cheever.

CHEEVER: I think it be my duty, sir – [*kindly, to* PROCTOR] You'll not deny it, John. [*To* DANFORTH] When we come to take his wife, he damned the court and ripped your warrant.

PARRIS: Now you have it!

DANFORTH: He did that, Mr Hale?

HALE [*takes a breath*]: Aye, he did.

PROCTOR: It were a temper, sir. I knew not what I did.

DANFORTH [*studying him*]: Mr Proctor.

PROCTOR: Aye, sir.

DANFORTH [*straight into his eyes*]: Have you ever seen the Devil?

PROCTOR: No, sir.

DANFORTH: You are in all respects a Gospel Christian?

2 **revelation**: uncovering of a surprising fact 8 **lurk**: lay hidden before you attack
19 **temper**: (here) sudden outburst of anger 24 **in all respects**: in every way
Gospel Christian: Christian person who follows religion faithfully

PROCTOR: I am, sir.

PARRIS: Such a Christian that will not come to church but once in a month!

DANFORTH [*restrained – he is curious*]: Not come to church?

PROCTOR: I – I have no love for Mr Parris. It is no secret. But God I surely love.

CHEEVER: He plough on Sunday, sir.

DANFORTH: Plough on Sunday!

CHEEVER [*apologetically*]: I think it be evidence, John. I am an official of the court, I cannot keep it.

PROCTOR: I – I have once or twice ploughed on Sunday. I have three children, sir, and until last year my land give little.

GILES: You'll find other Christians that do plough on Sunday, if the truth be known.

HALE: Your Honour, I cannot think you may judge the man on such evidence.

DANFORTH: I judge nothing. [*Pause. He keeps watching* PROCTOR, *who tries to meet his gaze.*] I tell you straight, Mister – I have seen marvels in this court. I have seen people choked before my eyes by spirits; I have seen them stuck by pins and slashed by daggers. I have until this moment not the slightest reason to suspect that the children may be deceiving me. Do you understand my meaning?

PROCTOR: Excellency, does it not strike upon you that so many of these women have lived so long with such upright reputation, and –

7 **plough** (v) **[plaʊ]**: dig over the earth in a field to prepare it for putting in seeds
9 **apologetically**: in a way that shows that you are sorry for sth. 18 **meet sb.'s gaze**: look sb. in the eye while they are looking at you 20 **slash sb.**: cut sb. **dagger**: knife

PARRIS: Do you read the Gospel, Mr Proctor?

PROCTOR: I read the Gospel.

PARRIS: I think not, or you should surely know that Cain were an upright man, and yet he did kill Abel.

PROCTOR: Ay, God tells us that. [*To* DANFORTH]: But who tells us Rebecca Nurse murdered seven babies by sending out her spirit on them? It is the children only, and this one will swear she lied to you.
[DANFORTH *considers, then beckons* HATHORNE *to him.* HATHORNE *leans in, and he speaks in his ear.* HATHORNE *nods.*]

HATHORNE: Aye, she's the one.

DANFORTH: Mr Proctor, this morning, your wife send me a claim in which she states that she is pregnant now.

PROCTOR: My wife pregnant!

DANFORTH: There be no sign of it – we have examined her body.

PROCTOR: But if she say she is pregnant, then she must be! That woman will never lie, Mr Danforth.

DANFORTH: She will not?

PROCTOR: Never, sir, never.

DANFORTH: We have thought it too convenient to be credited. However, if I should tell you now that I will let her be kept another month; and if she begin to show her natural signs, you shall have her living yet another year until she is delivered – what say you to that?
[JOHN PROCTOR *is struck silent.*]

12 **claim**: (here) statement submitted to court 20 **convenient**: good for you in a specific situation 23 **be delivered**: give birth 25 **be struck silent**: be unable to talk because of shock

Come now. You say your only purpose is to save your wife. Good, then, she is saved at least this year, and a year is long. What say you, sir? It is done now.
[*In conflict,* PROCTOR *glances at* FRANCIS *and* GILES.] Will you drop this charge?

PROCTOR: I – I think I cannot.

DANFORTH [*now an almost imperceptible hardness in his voice*]: Then your purpose is somewhat larger.

PARRIS: He's come to overthrow this court, Your Honour!

PROCTOR: These are my friends. Their wives are also accused –

DANFORTH [*with a sudden briskness of manner*]: I judge you not, sir. I am ready to hear your evidence.

PROCTOR: I come not to hurt the court; I only –

DANFORTH [*cutting him off*]: Marshal, go into the court and bid Judge Stoughton and Judge Sewall declare recess for one hour. And let them go to the tavern, if they will. All witnesses and prisoners are to be kept in the building.

HERRICK: Aye, sir. [*Very deferentially*] If I may say it, sir, I know this man all my life. It is a good man, sir.

DANFORTH [*it is the reflection on himself he resents*]: I am sure of it, Marshal.
[HERRICK *nods, then goes out.*] Now, what deposition do you have for us, Mr Proctor? And I beg you be clear, open as the sky, and honest.

PROCTOR [*as he takes out several papers*]: I am no lawyer, so I'll –

5 **drop a charge**: stop accusing sb. in court 7 **imperceptible**: unable to be noticed 11 **briskness**: quick and efficient way of behaving 14 **cut sb. off**: speak before sb. has finished speaking **Marshal**: court official whose function it is to make sure court business works well 15 **declare recess**: say that a trial will have a short pause 16 **tavern** (old-fashioned): pub 18 **deferentially**: respectfully 20 **sth.'s reflection on sb.**: what sth. tells us about sb.

DANFORTH: The pure in heart need no lawyers. Proceed as you will.

PROCTOR [*Handing* DANFORTH *a paper*]: Will you read this first, sir? It's a sort of testament. The people signing it declare their good opinion of Rebecca, and my wife, and Martha Corey.
[DANFORTH *looks down at the paper.*]

PARRIS [*to enlist* DANFORTH'S *sarcasm*]: Their good opinion! [*But* DANFORTH *goes on reading, and* PROCTOR *is heartened.*]

PROCTOR: These are all landholding farmers, members of the church. [*Delicately, trying to point out a paragraph*] If you'll notice, sir – they've known the women many years and never saw no sign they had dealings with the Devil.
[PARRIS *nervously moves over and reads over* DANFORTH'S *shoulder.*]

DANFORTH [*glancing down a long list*]: How many names are here?

FRANCIS: Ninety-one, Your Excellency.

PARRIS [*sweating*]: These people should be summoned.
[DANFORTH *looks up at him questioningly.*]
For questioning.

FRANCIS [*trembling with anger*]: Mr Danforth, I gave them all my word no harm would come to them for signing this.

PARRIS: This is a clear attack upon the court!

HALE [*to* PARRIS, *trying to contain himself*]: Is every defence an attack upon the court? Can no one – ?

PARRIS: All innocent and Christian people are happy for the courts in Salem! These people are gloomy for it. [*To* DANFORTH *directly*] And I think you will want to know, from each and every one of them, what discontents them with you!

3 **testament**: written statement for use in court 7 **heartened**: filled with hope 8 **landholding farmers**: farmers who own land 15 **summon sb.**: order sb. to appear at court 18–19 **give sb. your word**: make a promise to sb. 21 **contain yourself**: control your anger 24 **gloomy**: unhappy, depressed 26 **discontent sb. with sth.**: make sb. unhappy with sth.

HATHORNE: I think they ought to be examined, sir.

DANFORTH: It is not necessarily an attack, I think. Yet –

FRANCIS: These are all covenanted Christians, sir.

DANFORTH: Then I am sure they may have nothing to fear. [*Hands* CHEEVER *the paper*] Mr Cheever, have warrants drawn for all of these – arrest for examination. [*To* PROCTOR] Now, Mister, what other information do you have for us?
[FRANCIS *is still standing, horrified.*]
You may sit, Mr Nurse.

FRANCIS: I have brought trouble on these people; I have –

DANFORTH: No, old man, you have not hurt these people if they are of good conscience. But you must understand, sir, that a person is either with this court or he must be counted against it, there be no road between. This is a sharp time, now, a precise time – we live no longer in the dusky afternoon when evil mixed itself with good and befuddled the world. Now, by God's grace, the shining sun is up, and them that fear not light will surely praise it. I hope you will be one of those.
[MARY WARREN *suddenly sobs.*]
She's not hearty, I see.

PROCTOR: No, she's not, sir. [*To* MARY, *bending to her, holding her hand, quietly*] Now remember what the angel Raphael said to the boy Tobias. Remember it.

MARY WARREN [*hardly audible*]: Aye.

PROCTOR: 'Do that which is good, and no harm shall come to thee.'

MARY WARREN: Aye.

DANFORTH: Come, man, we wait you.

14 **sharp**: clearly defined **precise**: exact 15 **dusky**: quite dark 16 **befuddle sb.**: trick sb. 24 **audible**: loud enough to be heard 27 **we wait you** (old-fashioned): we wait for you

[MARSHAL HERRICK *returns, and takes his post at the door.*]

GILES: John, my deposition, give him mine.

PROCTOR: Aye. [*He hands* DANFORTH *another paper.*] This is Mr Corey's deposition.

DANFORTH: Oh? [*He looks down at it. Now* HATHORNE *comes behind him and reads with him.*]

HATHORNE [*suspiciously*]: What lawyer drew this, Corey?

GILES: You know I never hired a lawyer in my life, Hathorne.

DANFORTH [*finishing the reading*]: It is very well phrased. My compliments. Mr Parris, if Mr Putnam is in the court, will you bring him in?
[HATHORNE *takes the deposition, and walks to the window with it.* PARRIS *goes into the court.*] You have no legal training, Mr Corey?

GILES [*very pleased*]: I have the best, sir – I am thirty-three time in court in my life. And always plaintiff, too.

DANFORTH: Oh, then you're much put-upon.

GILES: I am never put-upon; I know my rights, sir, and I will have them. You know, your father tried a case of mine might be thirty-five year ago, I think.

DANFORTH: Indeed.

GILES: He never spoke to you of it?

DANFORTH: No, I cannot recall it.

GILES: That's strange, he give me nine pound damages. He were a fair judge, your father. Y'see, I had a white mare that time, and this fellow come to borrow the mare –

7 **suspiciously**: showing that you do not trust others **draw sth.**: write sth. (e.g. a legal text) 9 **well phrased**: well-written 13 **legal training**: study of the law 15 **plaintiff**: person who takes another person to court 16 **put-upon**: treated unfairly

[*Enter* PARRIS *with* THOMAS PUTNAM. *When he sees* PUTNAM, GILES' *ease goes; he is hard.*]
Aye, there he is.

DANFORTH: Mr Putnam, I have here an accusation by Mr Corey against you. He states that you coldly prompted your daughter to cry witchery upon George Jacobs that is now in jail.

PUTNAM: It is a lie.

DANFORTH [*turning to* GILES]: Mr Putnam states your charge is a lie. What say you to that?

GILES [*furious, his fists clenched*]: A fart on Thomas Putnam, that is what I say to that!

DANFORTH: What proof do you submit for your charge, sir?

GILES: My proof is there! [*Pointing to the paper*] If Jacobs hangs for a witch he forfeit up his property – that's law! And there is none but Putnam with the coin to buy so great a piece. This man is killing his neighbours for their land!

DANFORTH: But proof, sir, proof.

GILES [*pointing at his deposition*]: The proof is there! I have it from an honest man who heard Putnam say it! The day his daughter cried out on Jacobs, he said she'd given him a fair gift of land.

HATHORNE: And the name of this man?

GILES [*taken aback*]: What name?

HATHORNE: The man that give you this information.

GILES [*hesitates, then*]: Why, I – I cannot give you his name.

HATHORNE: And why not?

5 **prompt sb. to do sth.**: make sb. do sth. 6 **witchery**: witchcraft 10 **clench one's fists**: *die Faust ballen* **fart**: *Furz,* (here: used to express disrespect)
14 **forfeit sth. up**: lose sth. 22 **taken aback**: shocked

GILES [*hesitates, then bursts out*]: You know well why not! He'll lay in jail if I give his name!

HATHORNE: This is contempt of the court, Mr Danforth!

DANFORTH [*to avoid that*]: You will surely tell us the name.

GILES: I will not give you no name. I mentioned my wife's name once and I'll burn in hell long enough for that. I stand mute.

DANFORTH: In that case, I have no choice but to arrest you for contempt of this court, do you know that?

GILES: This is a hearing; you cannot clap me for contempt of a hearing.

DANFORTH: Oh, it is a proper lawyer! Do you wish me to declare the court in full session here? Or will you give me good reply?

GILES [*faltering*]: I cannot give you no name, sir, I cannot.

DANFORTH: You are a foolish old man. Mr Cheever, begin the record. The court is now in session. I ask you, Mr Corey –

PROCTOR [*breaking in*]: Your Honour – he has the story in confidence, sir, and he –

PARRIS: The Devil lives on such confidences [*To* DANFORTH] Without confidences there could be no conspiracy, Your Honour!

HATHORNE: I think it must be broken, sir.

DANFORTH [*to* GILES]: Old man, if your informant tells the truth let him come here openly like a decent man. But if he hide in anonymity I must know why. Now sir, the government and central church demand of you the name of him who reported Mr Thomas Putnam a common murderer.

6 **mute**: unable to speak 12 **in full session**: the actual trial, in which what is said is very important, as opposed to the less meaningful action in the anteroom
16–17 **have sth. in confidence**: be told sth. and promise not to reveal who said it
19 **conspiracy**: secret plan to harm others 25 **common**: ordinary, not special (here: morally low)

HALE: Excellency –

DANFORTH: Mr Hale.

HALE: We cannot blink it more. There is a prodigious fear of this court in the country –

DANFORTH: Then there is a prodigious guilt in the country. Are you afraid to be questioned here?

HALE: I may only fear the Lord, sir, but there is fear in the country nevertheless.

DANFORTH [*angered now*]: Reproach me not with the fear in the country; there is fear in the country because there is a moving plot to topple Christ in the country!

HALE: But it does not follow that everyone accused is part of it.

DANFORTH: No uncorrupted man may fear this court, Mr Hale! None! [*To* GILES] You are under arrest in contempt of this court. Now sit you down and take counsel with yourself, or you will be set in the jail until you decide to answer all questions.
[GILES COREY *makes a rush for* PUTNAM. PROCTOR *lunges and holds him.*]

PROCTOR: No, Giles!

GILES [*over* PROCTOR'S *shoulder at* PUTNAM]: I'll cut your throat, Putnam, I'll kill you yet!

PROCTOR [*forcing him into a chair*]: Peace, Giles, peace. [*Releasing him.*] We'll prove ourselves. Now we will. [*He starts to turn to* DANFORTH.]

GILES: Say nothin' more, John. [*Pointing at* DANFORTH] He's only playin' you! He means to hang us all!
[MARY WARREN *bursts into sobs.*]

9 **reproach sb.**: criticize sb. 13 **uncorrupted**: innocent 15 **take counsel with yourself**: think about your actions carefully 17 **lunge [lʌndʒ]**: throw yourself forward suddenly (e.g. to attack)

DANFORTH: This is a court of law, Mister. I'll have no effrontery here!

PROCTOR: Forgive him, sir, for his old age. Peace, Giles, we'll prove it all now. [*He lifts up* MARY'S *chin.*] You cannot weep, Mary. Remember the angel, what he say to the boy. Hold to it, now; there is your rock.
[MARY *quiets. He takes out a paper, and turns to* DANFORTH.] This is Mary Warren's deposition. I – I would ask you remember, sir, while you read it, that until two week ago she were no different than the other children are today. [*He is speaking reasonably, restraining all his fears, his anger, his anxiety.*] You saw her scream, she howled, she swore familiar spirits choked her; she even testified that Satan, in the form of women now in jail, tried to win her soul away, and then when she refused –

DANFORTH: We know all this.

PROCTOR: Aye, sir. She swears now that she never saw Satan; nor any spirit, vague or clear, that Satan may have sent to hurt her. And she declares her friends are lying now.
[PROCTOR *starts to hand* DANFORTH *the deposition, and* HALE *comes up to* DANFORTH *in a trembling state.*]

HALE: Excellency, a moment. I think this goes to the heart of the matter.

DANFORTH [*with deep misgivings*]: It surely does.

HALE: I cannot say he is an honest man; I know him little. But in all justice, sir, a claim so weighty cannot be argued by a farmer. In God's name, sir, stop here; send him home and let him come again with a lawyer –

DANFORTH [*patiently*]: Now look you, Mr Hale –

1 **effrontery**: extremely disrespectful behavior 6 **rock**: (here) person or thing that you can rely on 12 **howl**: (here) make a long, loud cry 17 **vague [veɪg]**: (here) unable to be seen clearly 21–22 **heart of the matter**: most important part of the situation

HALE: Excellency, I have signed seventy-two death warrants; I am a minister of the Lord, and I dare not take a life without there be a proof so immaculate no slightest qualm of conscience may doubt it.

DANFORTH: Mr Hale, you surely do not doubt my justice.

HALE: I have this morning signed away the soul of Rebecca Nurse, Your Honour. I'll not conceal it, my hand shakes yet as with a wound! I pray you, sir, *this* argument let lawyers present to you.

DANFORTH: Mr Hale, believe me; for a man of such terrible learning you are most bewildered – I hope you will forgive me. I have been thirty-two year at the bar, sir, and I should be confounded were I called upon to defend these people. Let you consider, now – [*To* PROCTOR *and the others*] And I bid you all do likewise. In an ordinary crime, how does one defend the accused? One calls up witnesses to prove his innocence. But witchcraft is *ipso facto*, on its face and by its nature, an invisible crime, is it not? Therefore, who may possibly be witness to it? The witch and the victim. None other. Now we cannot hope the witch will accuse herself; granted? Therefore, we must rely upon her victims – and they do testify, the children certainly do testify. As for the witches, none will deny that we are most eager for all their confessions. Therefore, what is left for a lawyer to bring out? I think I have made my point. Have I not?

HALE: But this child claims the girls are not truthful, and if they are not –

DANFORTH: That is precisely what I am about to consider, sir. What more may you ask of me? Unless you doubt my probity?

HALE [*defeated*]: I surely do not, sir. Let you consider it, then.

3 **immaculate [ɪ'mækjələt]**: (here) without any mistakes **qualm**: doubt
11 **be at the bar**: work as a lawyer **confounded**: strongly surprised 15–16 **ipso facto** (Lat.): in and of itself 19 **granted**: (here) used to make sure other people are of the same opinion **rely upon**: need 27 **probity**: honesty

DANFORTH: And let you put your heart to rest. Her deposition, Mr Proctor.

[PROCTOR *hands it to him.* HATHORNE *rises, goes beside* DANFORTH, *and starts reading.* PARRIS *comes to his other side.* DANFORTH *looks at* JOHN PROCTOR, *then proceeds to read.* HALE *gets up, finds position near the judge, reads too,* PROCTOR *glances at* GILES. FRANCIS *prays silently, hands pressed together.* CHEEVER *waits placidly, the sublime official, dutiful.* MARY WARREN *sobs once.* JOHN PROCTOR *touches her head reassuringly. Presently* DANFORTH *lifts his eyes, stands up, takes out a kerchief and blows his nose. The others stand aside as he moves in thought toward the window.*]

PARRIS [*hardly able to contain his anger and fear*]: I should like to question –

DANFORTH [*his first real outburst, in which his contempt for* PARRIS *is clear*]: Mr Parris, I bid you be silent! [*He stands in silence, looking out the window. Now, having established that be will set the gait*] Mr Cheever, will you go into the court and bring the children here?

[CHEEVER *gets up and goes out upstage.* DANFORTH *now turns to* MARY.]

Mary Warren, how came you to this turnabout? Has Mr Proctor threatened you for this deposition?

MARY WARREN: No, Sir.

DANFORTH: Has he ever threatened you?

MARY WARREN [*weaker*]: No, sir.

DANFORTH: [*sensing a weakening*]: Has he threatened you?

MARY WARREN: No, sir.

7 **placidly** ['plæsɪdli]: calmly **sublime**: (here) very good 8 **dutiful**: fulfilling what one is supposed to do 9 **reassuringly** [ˌriːə'ʃʊərɪŋli]: in a calming way
10 **kerchief** ['kɜːtʃɪf]: (here) short form of handkerchief 14 **outburst**: showing anger very suddenly 16 **set the gait**: control the speed of a procedure
18 **upstage**: back of the stage 20 **turnabout**: sudden, radical change

DANFORTH: Then you tell me that you sat in my court, callously lying, when you knew that people would hang by your evidence? [*She does not answer.*] Answer me!

MARY WARREN [*almost inaudibly*]: I did, sir.

DANFORTH: How were you instructed in your life? Do you not know that God damns all liars? [*She cannot speak.*] Or is it now that you lie?

MARY WARREN: No, sir – I am with God now.

DANFORTH: You are with God now.

MARY WARREN: Aye, sir.

DANFORTH [*containing himself*]: I will tell you this – you are either lying now, or you were lying in the court, and in either case you have committed perjury and you will go to jail for it. You cannot lightly say you lied, Mary. Do you know that?

MARY WARREN: I cannot lie no more. I am with God, I am with God. [*But she breaks into sobs at the thought of it, and the right door opens, and enter* SUSANNA WALCOTT, MERCY LEWIS, BETTY PARRIS, *and finally* ABIGAIL. CHEEVER *comes to* DANFORTH.]

CHEEVER: Ruth Putnam's not in the court, sir, nor the other children.

DANFORTH: These will be sufficient. Sit you down, children. [*Silently they sit.*] Your friend, Mary Warren, has given us a deposition. In which she swears that she never saw familiar spirits, apparitions, nor any manifest of the Devil. She claims as well that none of you have seen these things either. [*Slight pause.*] Now, children, this is a court of law. The law, based upon the Bible, and the Bible, writ

1 **callously**: without caring for the feelings of others 5 **inaudibly**: unable to be heard 15 **perjury**: the act of telling a lie in court 25 **apparition**: (here) ghost 28 **writ** (old-fashioned): written

by Almighty God, forbid the practice of witchcraft, and describe death as the penalty thereof. But likewise, children, the law and Bible damn all bearers of false witness. [*Slight pause*] Now then. It does not escape me that this deposition may be devised to blind us; it may well be that Mary Warren has been conquered by Satan, who sends her here to distract our sacred purpose. If so, her neck will break for it. But if she speak true, I bid you now drop your guile and confess your pretence, for a quick confession will go easier with you. [*Pause.*] Abigail Williams, rise.
[ABIGAIL *slowly rises.*]
Is there any truth in this?

ABIGAIL: No, sir.

DANFORTH [*thinks, glances at* MARY, *then back to* ABIGAIL]: Children, a very augur bit will now be turned into your souls until your honesty is proved. Will either of you change your positions now, or do you force me to hard questioning?

ABIGAIL: I have naught to change, sir. She lies.

DANFORTH [*to* MARY]: You would still go on with this?

MARY WARREN [*faintly*]: Aye, sir.

DANFORTH [*turning to* ABIGAIL]: A poppet were discovered in Mr Proctor's house, stabbed by a needle. Mary Warren claims that you sat beside her in the court when she made it, and that you saw her make it and witnessed how she herself stuck her needle into it for safe-keeping.What say you to that?

ABIGAIL [*with a slight note of indignation*]: It is a lie, sir.

DANFORTH [*after a slight pause*]: While you worked for Mr Proctor, did you see poppets in that house?

2 **penalty** ['penəlti]: punishment 4 **escape sb.**: (here) not be noticed by sb. **devise**: invent 5 **conquer sth./sb.**: take control of sth./sb. 6 **sacred**: holy 8 **guile** [gaɪl]: dishonest behaviour 14 **augur bit** ['ɔːgə(r) bɪt]: (auger bit) tip of a drill (here: the girls will be questioned very closely) 25 **indignation**: anger at a situation you think is unfair

ABIGAIL: Goody Proctor always kept poppets.

PROCTOR: Your Honour, my wife never kept no poppets. Mary Warren confesses it was her poppet.

CHEEVER: Your Excellency.

DANFORTH: Mr Cheever.

CHEEVER: When I spoke with Goody Proctor in that house, she said she never kept no poppets. But she said she did keep poppets when she were a girl.

PROCTOR: She has not been a girl these fifteen years, Your Honour.

HATHORNE: But a poppet will keep fifteen years, will it not?

PROCTOR: It will keep if it is kept, but Mary Warren swears she never saw no poppets in my house, nor anyone else.

PARRIS: Why could there not have been poppets hid where no one ever saw them?

PROCTOR [*furious*]: There might also be a dragon with five legs in my house, but no one has ever seen it.

PARRIS: We are here, Your Honour, precisely to discover what no one has ever seen.

PROCTOR: Mr Danforth, what profit this girl to turn herself about? What may Mary Warren gain but hard questioning and worse?

DANFORTH: You are charging Abigail Williams with a marvellous cool plot to murder, do you understand that?

PROCTOR: I do, sir. I believe she means to murder.

DANFORTH [*pointing at* ABIGAIL, *incredulously*]: This child would murder your wife?

1 **keep sth.**: (here) have sth. 15 **dragon**: *Drache* 24 **incredulously**: unable to believe what is happening 10 **keep**: (here) stay in good condition

PROCTOR: It is not a child. Now hear me, sir. In the sight of the congregation she were twice this year put out of this meetin' house for laughter during prayer.

DANFORTH [*shocked, turning to* ABIGAIL]: What's this? Laughter during – !

PARRIS: Excellency, she were under Tituba's power at that time, but she is solemn now.

GILES: Aye, now she is solemn and goes to hang people!

DANFORTH: Quiet, man.

HATHORNE: Surely it have no bearing on the question, sir. He charges contemplation of murder.

DANFORTH: Aye. [*He studies* ABIGAIL *for a moment, then*] Continue, Mr Proctor.

PROCTOR: Mary. Now tell the Governor how you danced in the woods.

PARRIS [*instantly*]: Excellency, since I come to Salem this man is blackening my name. He –

DANFORTH: In a moment, sir. [*To* MARY WARREN, *sternly, and surprised*] What is this dancing?

MARY WARREN: I – [*She glances at* ABIGAIL, *who is staring down at her remorselessly. Then, appealing to* PROCTOR] Mr Proctor –

PROCTOR [*taking it right up*]: Abigail leads the girls to the woods, Your Honour, and they have danced there naked –

PARRIS: Your Honour, this –

10 **have a bearing on sth.**: influence sth. 11 **contemplation**: (here) intention
18 **sternly**: seriously and strictly 21 **appeal to sb.**: asking sb. in a desperate way
22 **take sth. right up.**: answer straight away

PROCTOR [*at once*]: Mr Parris discovered them himself in the dead of night! There's the 'child' she is!

DANFORTH [*it is growing into a nightmare, and he turns, astonished, to* PARRIS]: Mr Parris –

PARRIS: I can only say, sir, that I never found any of them naked, and this man is –

DANFORTH: But you discovered them dancing in the woods? [*Eyes on* PARRIS, *he points at* ABIGAIL.] Abigail?

HALE: Excellency, when I first arrived from Beverly, Mr Parris told me that.

DANFORTH: Do you deny it, Mr Parris?

PARRIS: I do not, sir, but I never saw any of them naked.

DANFORTH: But she have *danced*?

PARRIS [*unwillingly*]: Aye, sir.
[DANFORTH, *as though with new eyes, looks at* ABIGAIL.]

HATHORNE: Excellency, will you permit me? [*He points at* MARY WARREN.]

DANFORTH [*with great worry*]: Pray, proceed.

HATHORNE: You say you never saw no spirits, Mary, were never threatened or afflicted by any manifest of the Devil or or the Devil's agents.

MARY WARREN [*very faintly*]: No, sir.

HATHORNE [*with a gleam of victory*]: And yet, when people accused of witchery confronted you in court, you would faint, saying their spirits came out of their bodies and choked you –

1–2 **in the dead of night**: in the middle of the night 3 **nightmare**: bad dream 16 **permit**: allow 20 **afflict sb.**: have a harmful effect on sb. 23 **gleam**: (here) showing a particular emotion on your face 24 **faint** (v): *ohnmächtig werden*

MARY WARREN: That were pretence, sir.

DANFORTH: I cannot hear you.

MARY WARREN: Pretence, sir.

PARRIS: But you did turn cold, did you not? I myself picked you up many times, and your skin were icy. Mr Danforth, you –

DANFORTH: I saw that many times.

PROCTOR: She only pretended to faint, Your Excellency. They're all marvellous pretenders.

HATHORNE: Then can she pretend to faint now?

PROCTOR: Now?

PARRIS: Why not? Now there are no spirits attacking her, for none in this room is accused of witchcraft. So let her turn herself cold now, let her pretend she is attacked now, let her faint. [*He turns to* MARY WARREN.] Faint!

MARY WARREN: Faint?

PARRIS: Aye, faint. Prove to us how you pretended in the court so many times.

MARY WARREN [*looking to* PROCTOR]: I – cannot faint now, sir.

PROCTOR [*alarmed, quietly*]: Can you not pretend it?

MARY WARREN: I – [*She looks about as though searching for the passion to faint.*] I – have no *sense* of it now, I –

DANFORTH: Why? What is lacking now?

MARY WARREN: I – cannot tell, sir, I –

DANFORTH: Might it be that here we have no afflicting spirit loose, but in the court there were some?

20 **passion**: (here) strong feeling 21 **sense**: (here) feeling 22 **be lacking**: be missing

MARY WARREN: I never saw no spirits.

PARRIS: Then see no spirits now, and prove to us that you can faint by your own will, as you claim.

MARY WARREN [*stares, searching for the emotion of it, and then shakes her head*]: I – cannot do it.

PARRIS: Then you will confess, will you not? It were attacking spirits made you faint!

MARY WARREN: No, sir, I –

PARRIS: Your Excellency, this is a trick to blind the court!

MARY WARREN: It's not a trick! [*She stands.*] I – I used to faint because I – I thought I saw spirits.

DANFORTH: *Thought* you saw them!

MARY WARREN: But I did not, Your Honour.

HATHORNE: How could you think you saw them unless you saw them?

MARY WARREN: I – I cannot tell how, but I did. I – I heard the other girls screaming, and you, Your Honour, you seemed to believe them, and I – It were only sport in the beginning, sir, but then the whole world cried spirits, spirits, and I – I promise you, Mr Danforth, I only thought I saw them but I did not.
[DANFORTH *peers at her.*]

PARRIS [*smiling, but nervous because* DANFORTH *seems to be struck by* MARY WARREN'S *story*]: Surely Your Excellency is not taken by this simple lie.

DANFORTH [*turning worriedly to* ABIGAIL]: Abigail. I bid you now search your heart and tell me this – and beware of it, child, to God every soul is precious and His vengeance is terrible on them that take life without cause. Is it possible, child, that the spirits

21 **peer at sb.**: look very closely at sb.

you have seen are illusion only, some deception that may cross your mind when –

ABIGAIL: Why, this – this – is a base question, sir.

DANFORTH : Child, I would have you consider it –

ABIGAIL: I have been hurt, Mr Danforth; I have seen my blood runnin' out! I have been near to murdered every day because I done my duty pointing out the Devil's people – and this is my reward? To be mistrusted, denied, questioned like a –

DANFORTH [*weakening*]: Child, I do not mistrust you –

ABIGAIL [*in an open threat*]: Let *you* beware, Mr Danforth. Think you to be so mighty that the power of Hell may not turn *your* wits? Beware of it! There is –
[*Suddenly, from an accusatory attitude, her face turns, looking into the air above – it is truly frightened.*]

DANFORTH [*apprehensively*]: What is it, child?

ABIGAIL [*looking about in the air, clasping her arms about her as though cold*]: I – I know not. A wind, a cold wind, has come. [*Her eyes fall on* MARY WARREN.]

MARY WARREN [*terrified, pleading*]: Abby!

MERCY LEWIS [*shivering*]: Your Honour, I freeze!

PROCTOR: They're pretending!

HATHORNE [*touching* ABIGAIL'S *hand*]: She is cold, Your Honour, touch her!

MERCY LEWIS [*through chattering teeth*]: Mary, do you send this shadow on me?

MARY WARREN: Lord, save me!

8 **deny sb.**: (here) doubt sb.'s good character 13 **accusatory**: showing that you think sb. has done sth. wrong 15 **apprehensively**: in a worried way 24 **chatter**: (of teeth) *zittern*

SUSANNA WALCOTT: I freeze, I freeze!

ABIGAIL [*shivering visibly*]: It is a wind, a wind!

MARY WARREN: Abby, don't do that!

DANFORTH [*himself engaged and entered by* ABIGAIL:] Mary Warren, do you witch her? I say to you, do you send your spirit out? [*With a hysterical cry,* MARY WARREN *starts to run.* PROCTOR *catches her.*]

MARY WARREN [*almost collapsing*]: Let me go, Mr Proctor. I cannot, I cannot –

ABIGAIL [*crying to Heaven*]: Oh, Heavenly Father, take away this shadow!
[*Without warning or hesitation,* PROCTOR *leaps at* ABIGAIL *and, grabbing her by the hair, pulls her to her feet. She screams in pain.* DANFORTH, *astonished, cries, 'What are you about?' and* HATHORNE *and* PARRIS *call, 'Take your hands of her!' and out of it all comes* PROCTOR'S *roaring voice.*]

PROCTOR: How do you call Heaven! Whore! Whore! [HERRICK *breaks* PROCTOR *from her.*]

HERRICK: John!

DANFORTH: Man! Man, what do you –

PROCTOR [*breathless and in agony*]: It is a whore!

DANFORTH [*dumbfounded*]: You charge – ?

ABIGAIL: Mr Danforth, he is lying!

PROCTOR: Mark her! Now she'll suck a scream to stab me with but –

DANFORTH: You will prove this! This will not pass!

4 **engage sb.**: attract sb.'s interest **enter sb.** (old-fashioned): have a strong influence on sb. 21 **agony**: great suffering 22 **dumbfounded**: so suprised that you cannot speak 24 **suck a scream** (old-fashioned): take in breath for a scream 25 **pass** (old use): (here) be accepted without challenge

PROCTOR [*trembling, his life collapsing about him*]: I have known her, sir. I have known her.

DANFORTH: You – you are a lecher?

FRANCIS [*horrified*]: John, you cannot say such a –

PROCTOR: Oh, Francis, I wish you had some evil in you that you might know me! [*To* DANFORTH] A man will not cast away his good name. You surely know that.

DANFORTH [*dumbfounded*]: In – in what time? In what place?

PROCTOR [*his voice about to break, and his shame great*]: In the proper place – where my beasts are bedded. On the last night of my joy, some eight months past. She used to serve me in my house, sir. [*He has to clamp his jaw to keep from weeping.*] A man may think God sleeps, but God sees everything, I know it now. I beg you, sir, I beg you – see her what she is. My wife, my dear good wife, took this girl soon after, sir, and put her out on the highroad. And being what she is, a lump of vanity, sir – [*He is being overcome.*] Excellency, forgive me, forgive me. [*Angrily against himself, he turns away from the Governor for a moment. Then, as though to cry out is his only means of speech left.*] She thinks to dance with me on my wife's grave! And well she might, for I thought of her softly. God help me, I lusted, and there is a promise in such sweat. But it is a whore's vengeance, and you must see it; I set myself entirely in your hands. I know you must see it now.

DANFORTH [*blanched, in horror, turning to* ABIGAIL]: You deny every scrap and tittle of this?

ABIGAIL: If I must answer that, I will leave and I will not come back again!
[DANFORTH *seems unsteady.*]

1 **know sb.** (old-fashioned): have sex with sb. 3 **lecher** (derog., old-fashioned): person with great need for sex 10 **bed sb.**: (here) give sb. a place to rest 16 **lump of vanity** (derog.): person who cares too much about what others think of them 20 **softly**: (here) with love 21 **lust** (v): desire sexually 24–25 **every scrap and tittle**: every last bit 28 **unsteady**: (here) not sure

PROCTOR: I have made a bell of my honour! I have rung the doom of my good name – you will believe me, Mr Danforth! My wife is innocent, except she knew a whore when she saw one!

ABIGAIL [*stepping up to* DANFORTH]: What look do you give me? [DANFORTH *cannot speak.*] I'll not have such looks! [*She turns and starts for the door.*]

DANFORTH: You will remain where you are! [HERRICK *steps into her path. She comes up short, fire in her eyes.*] Mr Parris, go into the court and bring Goodwife Proctor out.

PARRIS [*objecting*]: Your Honour, this is all a –

DANFORTH [*sharply to* PARRIS]: Bring her out! And tell her not one word of what's been spoken here. And let you knock before you enter. [PARRIS *goes out.*] Now we shall touch the bottom of this swamp. [*To* PROCTOR] Your wife, you say, is an honest woman.

PROCTOR: In her life, sir, she have never lied. There are them that cannot sing, and them that cannot weep – my wife cannot lie. I have paid much to learn it, sir.

DANFORTH: And when she put this girl out of your house, she put her out for a harlot?

PROCTOR: Aye, sir.

DANFORTH: And knew her for a harlot?

PROCTOR: Aye, sir, she knew her for a harlot.

DANFORTH: Good, then. [*To* ABIGAIL] And if she tell me, child, it were for harlotry, may God spread His mercy on you! [*There is a knock. He calls to the door.*] Hold! [*To* ABIGAIL] Turn your back. Turn your back. [*To* PROCTOR] Do likewise.

1 **make a bell of sth.**: (here) make publicly known **doom**: (here) destruction 8 **come up short**: stand still 10 **object** (v) [əb'dʒekt]: disagree 14 **swamp**: *Sumpf* 19 **harlot** (old-fashioned): prostitute 24 **harlotry** (old-fashioned): prostitution 25 **Hold!**: (here) Wait!

[*Both turn their backs* – ABIGAIL *with indignant slowness.*] Now let neither of you turn to face Goody Proctor. No one in this room is to speak one word, or raise a gesture aye or nay. [*He turns toward the door, calls*] Enter!
[*The door opens.* ELIZABETH *enters with* PARRIS. PARRIS *leaves her. She stands alone, her eyes looking for* PROCTOR.] Mr Cheever, report this testimony in all exactness. Are you ready?

CHEEVER: Ready, sir.

DANFORTH: Come here, woman. [ELIZABETH *comes to him, glancing at* PROCTOR'S *back.*] Look at me only, not at your husband. In my eyes only.

ELIZABETH [*faintly*]: Good, sir.

DANFORTH: We are given to understand that at one time you dismissed your servant, Abigail Williams.

ELIZABETH: That is true, sir.

DANFORTH: For what cause did you dismiss her?
[*Slight pause. Then* ELIZABETH *tries to glance at* PROCTOR.] You will look in my eyes only and not at your husband. The answer is in your memory and you need no help to give it to me. Why did you dismiss Abigail Williams?

ELIZABETH [*not knowing what to say, sensing a situation, wetting her lips to stall for time*]: She – dissatisfied me. [*Pause.*] And my husband.

DANFORTH: In what way dissatisfied you?

ELIZABETH: She were – [*She glances at* PROCTOR *for a cue.*]

DANFORTH: Woman, look at me! [ELIZABETH *does.*] Were she slovenly? Lazy? What disturbance did she cause?

3 **aye or nay** (old-fashioned) [**aɪ ɔː(r) neɪ**]: yes or no 18 **stall for time**: try to win some more time 25 **cue**: hint, sign 27 **slovenly** (adj): careless, untidy

ELIZABETH: Your Honour, I – in that time I were sick. And I – My husband is a good and righteous man. He is never drunk as some are, nor wastin' his time at the shovelboard, but always at his work. But in my sickness – you see, sir, I were a long time sick after my last baby, and I thought I saw my husband somewhat turning from me. And this girl –
[*She turns to* ABIGAIL.]

DANFORTH: Look at me.

ELIZABETH: Aye, sir. Abigail Williams – [*She breaks off.*]

DANFORTH: What of Abigail Williams?

ELIZABETH: I came to think he fancied her. And so one night I lost my wits, I think, and put her out on the highroad.

DANFORTH: Your husband – did he indeed turn from you?

ELIZABETH [*in agony*]: My husband – is a goodly man, sir.

DANFORTH: Then he did not turn from you.

ELIZABETH [*starting to glance at* PROCTOR]: He –

DANFORTH [*reaches out and holds her face, then*]: Look at me! To your own knowledge, has John Proctor ever committed the crime of lechery? [*In a crisis of indecision she cannot speak.*]
Answer my question! Is your husband a lecher!

ELIZABETH [*faintly*]: No, sir.

DANFORTH: Remove her, Marshal.

PROCTOR: Elizabeth, tell the truth!

DANFORTH: She has spoken. Remove her!

PROCTOR [*crying out*]: Elizabeth, I have confessed it!

2 **righteous** ['raɪtʃəs]: morally good 11 **fancy sb.**: find sb. attractive 11–12 **lose your wits.**: become angry 19 **indecision**: inability to decide

ELIZABETH: Oh, God!
[*The door closes behind her.*]

PROCTOR: She only thought to save my name!

HALE: Excellency, it is a natural lie to tell; I beg you, stop now before another is condemned! I may shut my conscience to it no more – private vengeance is working through this testimony! From the beginning this man has struck me true. By my oath to Heaven, I believe him now, and I pray you call back his wife before we –

DANFORTH: She spoke nothing of lechery, and this man has lied!

HALE: I believe him! [*Pointing at* ABIGAIL] This girl has always struck me false! She has –
[ABIGAIL, *with a weird, wild, chilling cry, screams up to the ceiling.*]

ABIGAIL: You will not! Begone! Begone, I say!

DANFORTH: What is it, child?
[*But* ABIGAIL, *pointing with fear, is now raising up her frightened eyes, her awed face, toward the ceiling – the girls are doing the same – and now* HATHORNE, HALE, PUTNAM, CHEEVER, HERRICK, *and* DANFORTH do *the same.*]
What's there? [*He lowers his eyes from the ceiling, and now he is frightened; there is real tension in his voice.*] Child!
[*She is transfixed – with all the girls, she is whimpering open-mouthed, agape at the ceiling.*]
Girls! Why do you – ?

MERCY LEWIS [*pointing*]: It's on the beam! Behind the rafter!

DANFORTH [*looking up*]: Where!

ABIGAIL: Why – ? [*She gulps.*] Why do you come, yellow bird?

7 **strike sb. true**: make sb. believe you **oath**: a statement that you swear is true 12 **weird [wɪəd]**: very strange **chilling**: making you feel cold (e.g. with fear) 16 **awed**: feeling a mixture of respect and fear 20 **tension**: (here) nervousness and fear 21 **transfixed**: unable to move because of great shock or surprise 22 **agape [ə'geɪp]**: with an open mouth

PROCTOR: Where's a bird? I see no bird!

ABIGAIL [*to the ceiling*]: My face? My face?

PROCTOR: Mr Hale –

DANFORTH: Be quiet!

PROCTOR [*to* HALE]: Do you see a bird?

DANFORTH: Be quiet!!

ABIGAIL [*to the ceiling, in a genuine conversation with the 'bird', as though trying to talk it out of attacking her*]: But God made my face; you cannot want to tear my face. Envy is a deadly sin, Mary.

MARY WARREN [*on her feet with a spring, and horrified, pleading*]: Abby!

ABIGAIL [*unperturbed, continuing to the 'bird'*]: Oh, Mary, this is a black art to change your shape. No, I cannot, I cannot stop my mouth; it's God's work I do.

MARY WARREN: Abby, I'm *here*!

PROCTOR [*frantically*]: They're pretending, Mr Danforth!

ABIGAIL [*now she takes a backward step, as though in fear the bird will swoop down momentarily*]: Oh, please, Mary! Don't come down.

SUSANNA WALCOTT: Her claws, she's stretching her claws!

PROCTOR: Lies, lies.

ABIGAIL [*backing farther, eyes still fixed above*]: Mary, please don't hurt me!

MARY WARREN [*to* DANFORTH]: I'm not hurting her!

DANFORTH [*to* MARY WARREN]: Why does she see this vision?

MARY WARREN: She sees nothin'!

7 **genuine**: real 10 **spring**: (here) quick, sudden jump 11 **unperturbed**: not disturbed 17 **swoop down**: fly down fast **momentarily**: (here) at any moment 18 **claw**: sharp nail on an animal's foot

ABIGAIL [*now staring full front as though hypnotized, and mimicking the exact tone of* MARY WARREN'S *cry*]: She sees nothin'!

MARY WARREN [*pleading*]: Abby, you mustn't!

ABIGAIL AND ALL THE GIRLS [*all transfixed*]: Abby, you mustn't!

MARY WARREN [*to all the girls*]: I'm here, I'm here!

GIRLS: I'm here, I'm here!

DANFORTH [*horrified*]: Mary Warren! Draw back your spirit out of them!

MARY WARREN: Mr Danforth!

GIRLS [*cutting her off*]: Mr Danforth!

DANFORTH: Have you compacted with the Devil? Have you?

MARY WARREN: Never, never!

GIRLS: Never, never!

DANFORTH [*growing hysterical*]: Why can they only repeat you?

PROCTOR: Give me a whip – I'll stop it!

MARY WARREN: They're sporting. They – !

GIRLS: They're sporting!

MARY WARREN [*turning on them all, hysterically and stamping her feet*]: Abby, stop it!

GIRLS [*stamping their feet*]: Abby, stop it!

MARY WARREN: Stop it!

GIRLS: Stop it!

MARY WARREN [*screaming it out at the top of her lungs, and raising her fists*]: Stop it!!

GIRLS [*raising their fists*]: Stop it!!

[MARY WARREN, *utterly confounded, and becoming overwhelmded by* ABIGAIL'S *– and the girls' – utter conviction, starts to whimper, hands half raised, powerless, and all the girls begin whimpering exactly as she does.*]

DANFORTH: A little while ago you were afflicted. Now it seems you afflict others; where did you find this power?

MARY WARREN [*staring at* ABIGAIL]: I – have no power.

GIRLS: I have no power.

PROCTOR: They're gulling you, Mister!

DANFORTH: Why did you turn about this past two weeks? You have seen the Devil, have you not?

HALE [*indicating* ABIGAIL *and the girls*]: You cannot believe them!

MARY WARREN: I –

PROCTOR [*sensing her weakening*]: Mary, God damns all liars!

DANFORTH [*pounding it into her*]: You have seen the Devil, you have made compact with Lucifer, have you not?

PROCTOR: God damns liars, Mary!

[MARY *utters something unintelligible, staring at* ABIGAIL, *who keeps watching the 'bird' above.*]

DANFORTH: I cannot hear you. What do you say?

[MARY *utters again unintelligibly*.]

You will confess yourself or you will hang! [*He turns her roughly to face him.*] Do you know who I am? I say you will hang if you do not open with me!

2 **utterly** (adj): completely **overwhelmed**: completely overcome with sth.
3 **conviction**: (here) appearance of real belief 9 **gull sb.**: deceive sb. 15 **pound sth. into sb.**: saying sth. repeatedly and forcefully to sb., as if hitting them with the words 18 **utter sth.**: say sth. quietly **unintelligible**: impossible to understand

PROCTOR: Mary, remember the angel Raphael – do that which is good and –

ABIGAIL [*pointing upward*]: The wings! Her wings are spreading! Mary, please, don't, don't – !

HALE: I see nothing, Your Honour!

DANFORTH: Do you confess this power! [*He is an inch from her face.*] Speak!

ABIGAIL: She's going to come down! She's walking the beam!

DANFORTH: Will you speak!

MARY WARREN [*staring in horror*]: I cannot!

GIRLS: I cannot!

PARRIS: Cast the Devil out! Look him in the face! Trample him! We'll save you, Mary, only stand fast against him and –

ABIGAIL [*looking up*]: Look out! She's coming down!
[*She and all the girls run to one wall, shielding their eyes. And now, as though cornered, they let out a gigantic scream, and* MARY, *as though infected, opens her mouth and screams with them. Gradually* ABIGAIL *and the girls leave off, until only* MARY *is left there, staring up at the 'bird', screaming madly. All watch her, horrified by this evident fit.* PROCTOR *strides to her.*]

PROCTOR: Mary, tell the Governor what they – [*He has hardly got a word out, when, seeing him coming for her, she rushes out of his reach, screaming in horror.*]

MARY WARREN: Don't touch me – don't touch me!
[*At which the girls halt at the door.*]

PROCTOR [*astonished*]: Mary!

12 **trample sth./sb.**: destroy sth. or sb. by stepping on it/them hard 13 **stand fast against sth**: not be influenced by sth. 15 **shield**: protect 16 **cornered**: pushed into a corner from where you cannot escape 17 **infect sb.**: (here) make sb. do or feel the same as you

MARY WARREN [*pointing at* PROCTOR]: You're the Devil's man! [*He is stopped in his tracks.*]

PARRIS: Praise God!

GIRLS: Praise God!

PROCTOR [*numbed*]: Mary, how – ?

MARY WARREN: I'll not hang with you! I love God, I love God.

DANFORTH [*to* MARY]: He bid you do the Devil's work?

MARY WARREN [*hysterically, indicating* PROCTOR]: He come at me by night and every day to sign, to sign, to –

DANFORTH: Sign what?

PARRIS: The Devil's book? He come with a book?

MARY WARREN [*hysterically, pointing at* PROCTOR, *fearful of him*]: My name, he want my name. 'I'll murder you', he says, 'if my wife hangs! We must go and overthrow the court,' he says! [DANFORTH'S *head jerks toward* PROCTOR, *shock and horror in his face.*]

PROCTOR [*turning, appealing to* HALE]: Mr Hale!

MARY WARREN [*her sobs beginning*]: He wake me every night, his eyes were like coals and his fingers claw my neck, and I sign, I sign …

HALE: Excellency, this child's gone wild!

PROCTOR [*as* DANFORTH'S *wide eyes pour on him*]: Mary, Mary!

MARY WARREN [*screaming at him*]: No, I love God; I go your way no more. I love God, I bless God. [*Sobbing, she rushes to* ABIGAIL.] Abby, Abby, I'll never hurt you more!

2 **stop in your tracks**: come to a sudden stop 9 **hysterically**: in a crazy way 5 **numbed**: unable to feel or move in a normal way 15 **jerk**: make a sudden, quick movement 19 **claw** (v): grab hard, digging your fingernails in

[*They all watch, as* ABIGAIL, *out of her infinite charity, reaches out and draws the sobbing* MARY *to her, and then looks up to* DANFORTH.]

DANFORTH [*to* PROCTOR]: What are you? [PROCTOR *is beyond speech in his anger.*] You are combined with anti-Christ, are you not? I have seen your power; you will not deny it! What say you, Mister?

HALE: Excellency –

DANFORTH: I will have nothing from you, Mr Hale! [*To* PROCTOR] Will you confess yourself befouled with Hell, or do you keep that black allegiance yet? What say you?

PROCTOR [*his mind wild, breathless*]: I say – I say – God is dead!

PARRIS: Hear it, hear it!

PROCTOR [*laughs insanely, then*]: A fire, a fire is burning! I hear the boot of Lucifer, I see his filthy face! And it is my face, and yours, Danforth! For them that quail to bring men out of ignorance, as I have quailed, and as you quail now when you know in all your black hearts that this be fraud – God damns our kind especially, and we will burn, we will burn together!

DANFORTH: Marshal! Take him and Corey with him to the jail!

HALE [*starting across to the door*]: I denounce these proceedings!

PROCTOR: You are pulling Heaven down and raising up a whore!

HALE: I denounce these proceedings, I quit this court! [*He slams the door to the outside behind him.*]

DANFORTH [*calling to him in a fury*]: Mr Hale! Mr Hale!

THE CURTAIN FALLS

8 **befouled**: made dirty 9 **allegiance**: loyalty 12 **insanely**: crazily
19 **denounce**: say clearly that you think sth. is wrong 21 **quit**: leave
21–22 **slam a door**: shut a door very loudly 23 **in a fury**: with great anger

ACT FOUR

A cell in Salem jail, that fall.

At the back is a high barred window; near it, a great, heavy door. Along the walls are two benches.

The place is in darkness but for the moonlight seeping through the bars. It appears empty. Presently footsteps are heard coming down a corridor beyond the wall, keys rattle, and the door swings open. MARSHAL HERRICK *enters with a lantern.*

He is nearly drunk, and heavy-footed. He goes to a bench and nudges a bundle of rags lying on it.

HERRICK: Sarah, wake up! Sarah Good! [*He then crosses to the other bench.*]

SARAH GOOD [*rising in her rags*]: Oh, Majesty! Comin', comin'! Tituba, he's here, His Majesty's come!

HERRICK: Go to the north cell; this place is wanted now. [*He hangs his lantern on the wall.* TITUBA *sits up.*]

TITUBA: That don't look to me like His Majesty; look to me like the marshal.

HERRICK [*taking out a flask*]: Get along with you now, clear this place. [*He drinks, and* SARAH GOOD *comes and peers up into his face.*]

SARAH GOOD: Oh, is it you, Marshal! I thought sure you be the devil comin' for us. Could I have a sip of cider for me goin'-away?

HERRICK [*handing her the flask*]: And where are you off to, Sarah?

1 **fall** (AE): autumn 2 **barred**: with metal sticks to stop people coming through (of windows or doors) 4 **seep**: flow slowly 5 **bar**: metal stick over a window or door 8–9 **nudge sb.**: get sb.'s attention by pushing them slightly 9 **rag**: piece of old cloth 18 **flask**: bottle 22 **sip** (n): small amount of liquid that you drink

TITUBA [*as* SARAH *drinks*]: We goin' to Barbados, soon the Devil gits here with the feathers and the wings.

HERRICK: Oh? A happy voyage to you.

SARAH GOOD: A pair of bluebirds wingin' southerly, the two of us! Oh, it be a grand transformation, Marshal! [*She raises the flask to drink again.*]

HERRICK [*taking the flask from her lips*]: You'd best give me that or you'll never rise off the ground. Come along now.

TITUBA: I'll speak to him for you, if you desires to come along, Marshal.

HERRICK: I'd not refuse it, Tituba; it's the proper morning to fly into Hell.

TITUBA: Oh, it be no Hell in Barbados. Devil, him be pleasure-man in Barbados, him be singin' and dancin' in Barbados. It's you folks – you riles him up 'round here; it be too cold 'round here for that Old Boy. He freeze his soul in Massachusetts, but in Barbados he just as sweet and –
[*A bellowing cow is heard, and* TITUBA *leaps us and calls to the window*]
Aye, sirs That's him, Sarah!

SARAH GOOD: I'm here, Majesty!
[*They hurriedly pick up their rags as* HOPKINS, *a guard, enters.*]

HOPKINS: The Deputy Governor's arrived.

HERRICK [*grabbing* TITUBA]: Come along, come along.

TITUBA [*resisting him*]: No, he comin' for me. I goin' home!

1 **gits**: (dialect) gets 4 **bluebird**: *Hüttensänger (nordamerikanischer Singvogel)* **wing** (v): fly **southerly**: South 5 **transformation**: change 15 **rile sb. up**: make sb. very angry 18 **bellow**: loud, deep sound

HERRICK [*pulling her to the door*]: That's not Satan, just a poor old cow with a hatful of milk. Come along now, out with you!

TITUBA [*calling to the window*]: Take me home, Devil! Take me home!

SARAH GOOD [*following the shouting* TITUBA *out*]: Tell him I'm goin', Tituba! Now you tell him Sarah Good is goin' too! [*In the corridor outside* TITUBA *calls on – 'Take me home, Devil; Devil take me home!' and* HOPKINS'S *voice orders her to move on.* HERRICK *returns and begins to push old rags and straw into a corner. Hearing footsteps, he turns, and enter* DANFORTH *and* JUDGE HATHORNE. *They are in greatcoats and wear hats against the bitter cold. They are followed in by* CHEEVER, *who carries a dispatch case and a flat wooden box containing his writing materials.*]

HERRICK: Good morning, Excellency.

DANFORTH: Where is Mr Parris?

HERRICK: I'll fetch him [*He starts for the door.*]

DANFORTH: Marshal.
[HERRICK *stops.*]
When did Reverend Hale arrive?

HERRICK: It were toward midnight, I think.

DANFORTH [*suspiciously*]: What is he about here?

HERRICK: He goes among them that will hang, sir. And he prays with them. He sits with Goody Nurse now. And Mr Parris with him.

DANFORTH: Indeed. That man have no authority to enter here, Marshal. Why have you let him in?

HERRICK: Why, Mr Parris command me, sir. I cannot deny him.

DANFORTH: Are you drunk, Marshal?

2 **hatful of milk**: with an udder *(Euter)* full of milk   10 **greatcoat**: a long, thick coat   11 **dispatch case**: briefcase used for carrying official documents

HERRICK: No, sir; it is a bitter night, and I have no fire here.

DANFORTH [*containing his anger*]: Fetch Mr Parris.

HERRICK: Aye, sir.

DANFORTH: There is a prodigious stench in this place.

HERRICK: I have only now cleared the people out for you.

DANFORTH: Beware hard drink, Marshal.

HERRICK: Aye, sir. [*He waits an instant for further orders. But* DANFORTH, *in dissatisfaction, turns his back on him, and* HERRICK *goes out. There is a pause.* DANFORTH *stands in thought.*]

HATHORNE: Let you question Hale, Excellency; I should not be surprised he have been preaching in Andover lately.

DANFORTH: We'll come to that; speak nothing of Andover. Parris prays with him. That's strange. [*He blows on his hands, moves toward the window, and looks out.*]

HATHORNE: Excellency, I wonder if it be wise to let Mr Parris so continuously with the prisoners. [DANFORTH *turns to him, interested.*] I think, sometimes, the man has a mad look these days.

DANFORTH: Mad?

HATHORNE: I met him yesterday coming out of his house, and I bid him good morning – and he wept and went his way. I think it is not well the village sees him so unsteady.

DANFORTH: Perhaps he have some sorrow.

CHEEVER [*stamping his feet against the cold*]: I think it be the cows, sir.

DANFORTH: Cows?

CHEEVER: There be so many cows wanderin' the highroads, now their masters are in the jails, and much disagreement who they

4 **stench**: very bad smell

will belong to now. I know Mr Parris be arguin' with farmers all yesterday – there is great contention, sir, about the cows. Contention make him weep, sir; it were always a man that weep for contention. [*He turns, as do* HATHORNE *and* DANFORTH, *hearing someone coming up the corridor.* DANFORTH *raises his head as* PARRIS *enters. He is gaunt, frightened, and sweating in his greatcoat.*]

PARRIS [*to* DANFORTH, *instantly*]: Oh, good morning, sir, thank you for coming, I beg your pardon wakin' you so early. Good morning, Judge Hathorne.

DANFORTH: Reverend Hale have no right to enter this –

PARRIS: Excellency, a moment. [*He hurries back and shuts the door.*]

HATHORNE: Do you leave him alone with the prisoners?

DANFORTH: What's his business here?

PARRIS [*prayerfully holding up his hands*]: Excellency, hear me. It is a providence. Reverend Hale has returned to bring Rebecca Nurse to God.

DANFORTH [*surprised*]: He bids her confess?

PARRIS [*sitting*]: Hear me. Rebecca have not given me a word this three month since she came. Now she sits with him, and her sister and Martha Corey and two or three others, and he pleads with them, confess their crimes and save their lives.

DANFORTH: Why – this is indeed a providence. And they soften, they soften?

PARRIS: Not yet, not yet. But I thought to summon you, sir, that we might think on whether it be not wise, to – [*He dares not say it.*] I had thought to put a question, sir, and I hope you will not –

DANFORTH: Mr Parris, be plain, what troubles you?

6 **gaunt**: pale and thin, from illness or worry 20 **plead with sb.**: beg sb. very seriously

PARRIS: There is news, sir, that the court – the court must reckon with. My niece, sir, my niece – I believe she has vanished.

DANFORTH: Vanished!

PARRIS: I had thought to advise you of it earlier in the week, but –

DANFORTH: Why? How long is she gone?

PARRIS: This be the third night. You see, sir, she told me she would stay a night with Mercy Lewis. And next day, when she does not return, I send to Mr Lewis to inquire. Mercy told him she would sleep in my house for a night.

DANFORTH: They are both gone?!

PARRIS [*in fear of him*]: They are, sir.

DANFORTH [*alarmed*]: I will send a party for them. Where may they be?

PARRIS: Excellency, I think they be aboard a ship.
[DANFORTH *stands agape.*]
My daughter tells me how she heard them speaking of ships last week, and tonight I discover my – my strongbox is broke into. [*He presses his fingers against his eyes to keep back tears.*]

HATHORNE [*astonished*]: She have robbed you?

PARRIS: Thirty-one pound is gone. I am penniless. [*He covers his face and sobs.*]

DANFORTH: Mr Parris, you are a brainless man! [*He walks in thought, deeply worried.*]

PARRIS: Excellency, it profit nothing you should blame me. I cannot think they would run off except they fear to keep in Salem any more. [*He is pleading.*] Mark it, sir, Abigail had close knowledge of the town, and since the news of Andover has broken here –

12 **party**: (here) group of people who search for sb. 17 **strongbox**: box that can be locked, in which to keep money and other valuables

DANFORTH: Andover is remedied. The court returns there on Friday, and will resume examinations.

PARRIS: I am sure of it, sir. But the rumour here speaks rebellion in Andover, and it –

DANFORTH: There is no rebellion in Andover!

PARRIS: I tell you what is said here, sir. Andover have thrown out the court, they say, and will have no part of witchcraft. There be a faction here, feeding on that news, and I tell you true, sir, I fear there will be riot here.

HATHORNE: Riot! Why at every execution I have seen naught but high satisfaction in the town.

PARRIS: Judge Hathorne – it were another sort that hanged till now. Rebecca Nurse is no Bridget that lived three year with Bishop before she married him. John Proctor is not Isaac Ward that drank his family to ruin. [*To* DANFORTH] I would to God it were not so, Excellency, but these people have great weight yet in the town. Let Rebecca stand upon the gibbet and send up some righteous prayer, and I fear she'll wake a vengeance on you.

HATHORNE: Excellency, she is condemned a witch. The court have –

DANFORTH: [*in deep concern, raising a hand to* HATHORNE]: Pray you. [*To* PARRIS] How do you propose, then?

PARRIS: Excellency, I would postpone these hangin's for a time.

DANFORTH: There will be no postponement.

PARRIS: Now Mr Hale's returned, there is hope, I think – for if he bring even one of these to God, that confession surely damns the others in the public eye, and none may doubt more that they are

1 **remedy sth.**: fix a bad situation 2 **resume sth.**: start sth. again 7 **have no part of sth.**: have nothing to do with sth. 8 **feed on sth.**: get strength from sth.
17 **gibbet** (old-fashioned) **['dʒɪbɪt]**: wooden structure used for hanging people
21 **How do you propose?** (old-fashioned): What do you suggest? 23 **postponement**: delay

all linked to Hell. This way, unconfessed and claiming innocence, doubts are multiplied, many honest people will weep for them, and our good purpose is lost in their tears.

DANFORTH [*after thinking a moment, then going to* CHEEVER]: Give me the list.
[CHEEVER *opens the dispatch case, searches.*]

PARRIS: It cannot be forgot, sir, that when I summoned the congregation for John Proctor's excommunication there were hardly thirty people come to hear it. That speak a discontent, I think, and –

DANFORTH [*studying the list*]: There will be no postponement.

PARRIS: Excellency –

DANFORTH: Now, sir – which of these in your opinion may be brought to God? I will myself strive with him till dawn. [*He hands the list to* PARRIS, *who merely glances at it.*]

PARRIS: There is not sufficient time till dawn.

DANFORTH: I shall do my utmost. Which of them do you have hope for?

PARRIS [*not even glancing at the list now, and in a quavering voice, quietly*]: Excellency – a dagger – [*He chokes up.*]

DANFORTH: What do you say?

PARRIS: Tonight, when I open my door to leave my house – a dagger clattered to the ground. [*Silence.* DANFORTH *absorbs this. Now* PARRIS *cries out.*] You cannot hang this sort. There is danger for me. I dare not step outside at night!
[REVEREND HALE *enters. They look at him for an instant in silence. He is steeped in sorrow, exhausted, and more direct than he ever was.*]

8 **excommunication**: punish sb. by not letting them be a member of church
17 **do your utmost**: do the best you can 20 **choke up**: be unable to speak because of a strong emotion 23 **clatter**: (of hard objects) make a loud noise 27 **steeped in sorrow**: extremely sad **exhausted**: very tired

DANFORTH: Accept my congratulations, Reverend Hale; we are gladdened to see you returned to your good work.

HALE [*Coming to* DANFORTH now]: You must pardon them. They will not budge.
[HERRICK *enters, waits.*]

DANFORTH [*conciliatory*]: You misunderstand, sir; I cannot pardon these when twelve are already hanged for the same crime. It is not just.

PARRIS [*with failing heart*]: Rebecca will not confess?

HALE: The sun will rise in a few minutes. Excellency, I must have more time.

DANFORTH: Now hear me, and beguile yourselves no more. I will not receive a single plea for pardon or postponement. Them that will not confess will hang. Twelve are already executed; the names of these seven are given out, and the village expects to see them die this morning. Postponement now speaks a floundering on my part; reprieve or pardon must cast doubt upon the guilt of them that died till now. While I speak God's law, I will not crack its voice with whimpering. If retaliation is your fear, know this – I should hang ten thousand that dared to rise against the law, and an ocean of salt tears could not melt the resolution of the statutes. Now draw yourselves up like men and help me, as you are bound by Heaven to do. Have you spoken with them all, Mr Hale?

HALE: All but Proctor. He is in the dungeon.

DANFORTH [*to* HERRICK]: What's Proctor's way now?

2 **gladdened**: happy 3 **pardon sb.**: forgive sb. 6 **conciliatory [kən'sɪliətəri]**: trying to make sb. stop fighting with you 8 **just**: fair 12 **beguile yourself [bɪ'gaɪl]**: deceive yourself 16 **flounder ['flaʊndə(r)]**: (here) be unsure of one's decision 17 **reprieve**: cancel a punishment **cast doubt upon sth.**: make people feel unsure about sth. 19 **retaliation [rɪˌtæli'eɪʃn]**: revenge 21 **statute**: law 24 **dungeon ['dʌndʒən]**: dark, underground prison

HERRICK: He sits like some great bird; you'd not know he lived except he will take food from time to time.

DANFORTH [*after thinking a moment*]: His wife – his wife must be well on with child now.

HERRICK: She is, sir.

DANFORTH: What think you, Mr Parris? You have closer knowledge of this man; might her presence soften him?

PARRIS: It is possible, sir. He have not laid eyes on her these three months. I should summon her.

DANFORTH [*to* HERRICK]: Is he yet adamant? Has he struck at you again?

HERRICK: He cannot, sir, he is chained to the wall now.

DANFORTH [*after thinking on it*]: Fetch Goody Proctor to me. Then let you bring him up.

HERRICK: Aye, sir. [HERRICK *goes. There is silence.*]

HALE: Excellency, if you postpone a week and publish to the town that you are striving for their confessions, that speak mercy on your part, not faltering.

DANFORTH: Mr Hale, as God have not empowered me like Joshua to stop this sun from rising, so I cannot withhold from them the perfection of their punishment.

HALE [*harder now*]: If you think God wills you to raise rebellion, Mr Danforth, you are mistaken!

DANFORTH [*instantly*]: You have heard rebellion spoken in the town?

3–4 **be well on with child** (old-fashioned): be in an advanced state of pregnancy 10 **adamant** ['ædəmənt]: very sure of your opinion 19 **empower sb. to do sth.**: give sb. the power to do sth. 20 **withhold sth. from sb.**: not give sth. to sb. 21 **perfection of sth.**: (here) act of carrying sth. out 22 **will sb to do sth.** (old-fashioned): want sb. to do sth.

HALE: Excellency, there are orphans wandering from house to house; abandoned cattle bellow on the highroads, the stink of rotting crops hangs everywhere, and no man knows when the harlots' cry will end his life – and you wonder yet if rebellion's spoke? Better you should marvel how they do not burn your province!

DANFORTH: Mr Hale, have you preached in Andover this month?

HALE: Thank God they have no need of me in Andover.

DANFORTH: You baffle me, sir. Why have you returned here?

HALE: Why, it is all simple. I come to do the Devil's work. I come to counsel Christians they should belie themselves. [*His sarcasm collapses.*] There is blood on my head! Can you not see the blood on my head!!

PARRIS: Hush! [*For he has heard footsteps. They all face the door.* HERRICK *enters with* ELIZABETH. *Her wrists are linked by heavy chain, which* HERRICK *now removes. Her clothes are dirty; her face is pale and gaunt.* HERRICK *goes out.*]

DANFORTH: [*very politely*]: Goody Proctor.
[*She is silent.*]
I hope you are hearty?

ELIZABETH [*as a warning reminder*]: I am yet six month before my time.

DANFORTH: Pray be at your ease, we come not for your life. We – [*uncertain bow to plead, for he is not accustomed to it.*] Mr Hale, will you speak with the woman?

HALE: Goody Proctor, your husband is marked to hang this morning.
[*Pause.*]

1 **orphan**: child whose parents are dead 4 **if rebellion's spoke**: if rebellion is spoken of 8 **baffle sb.**: make sb. confused 10 **belie yourself**: give a false impression of yourself 20 **reminder**: sth. that makes you remember 23 **be accustomed to sth**: be used to sth. 25 **mark sb. to do sth.**: decide that sb. has to do sth.

ELIZABETH [*quietly*]: I have heard it.

HALE: You know, do you not, that I have no connection with the court? [*She seems to doubt it.*] I come of my own, Goody Proctor. I would save your husband's life, for if he is taken I count myself his murderer. Do you understand me?

ELIZABETH: What do you want of me?

HALE: Goody Proctor, I have gone this three month like our Lord into the wilderness. I have sought a Christian way, for damnation's doubled on a minister who counsels men to lie.

HATHORNE: It is no lie, you cannot speak of lies.

HALE: It is a lie! They are innocent!

DANFORTH: I'll hear no more of that!

HALE [*continuing to* ELIZABETH]: Let you not mistake your duty as I mistook my own. I came into this village like a bridegroom to his beloved, bearing gifts of high religion; the very crowns of holy law I brought, and what I touched with my bright confidence, it died; and where I turned the eye of my great faith, blood flowed up. Beware, Goody Proctor – cleave to no faith when faith brings blood. It is mistaken law that leads you to sacrifice. Life, woman, life is God's most precious gift; no principle, however glorious, may justify the taking of it. I beg you, woman, prevail upon your husband to confess. Let him give his lie. Quail not before God's judgement in this, for it may well be God damns a liar less than he that throws his life away for pride. Will you plead with him? I cannot think he will listen to another.

ELIZABETH [*quietly*]: I think that be the Devil's argument.

4–5 **count yourself sth.**: see yourself as sth. 14 **bridegroom**: man who will get married 18 **cleave to sth.**: hold on to sth. tightly 19 **sacrifice sth.**: (here) kill sth. that is important to you 21 **prevail upon sb. to do sth.**: try to make sb. do sth. by trying to convice them

HALE [*with a climactic desperation*]: Woman, before the laws of God we are as swine! We cannot read His will!

ELIZABETH: I cannot dispute with you, sir; I lack learning for it.

DANFORTH [*going to her*]: Goody Proctor, you are not summoned here for disputation. Be there no wifely tenderness within you? He will die with the sunrise. Your husband. Do you understand it? [*She only looks at him.*] What say you? Will you contend with him? [*She is silent.*] Are you stone? I tell you true, woman, had I no other proof of your unnatural life, your dry eyes now would be sufficient evidence that you delivered up your soul to Hell! A very ape would weep at such calamity! Have the devil dried up any tear of pity in you? [*She is silent.*] Take her out. It profit nothing she should speak to him!

ELIZABETH [*quietly*]: Let me speak with him, Excellency.

PARRIS [*with hope*]: You'll strive with him?
[*She hesitates.*]

DANFORTH: Will you plead for his confession or will you not?

ELIZABETH: I promise nothing. Let me speak with him. [*A sound – the sibilance of dragging feet on stone. They turn. A pause.* HERRICK *enters with* JOHN PROCTOR. *His wrists are chained. He is another man, bearded, filthy, his eyes misty as though webs had overgrown them. He halts inside the doorway, his eye caught by the sight of* ELIZABETH. *The emotion flowing between them prevents anyone from speaking for an instant. Now* HALE, *visibly affected, goes to* DANFORTH *and speaks quietly.*]

HALE: Pray, leave them, Excellency.

1 **climactic**: (here) getting very strong 2 **swine** (pl.: swine): pig 3 **dispute**: debate 5 **disputation**: intellectual discussion 7 **contend with sb.**: (here) argue with sb. 10 **deliver sth. up**: let sb. else control sth. 11 **ape**: large monkey 19 **sibilance**: hissing sound **dragging feet**: when feet are not lifted from the floor while walking 21 **misty**: unclear **web**: spider's web

DANFORTH [*pressing* HALE *impatiently aside*]: Mr Proctor, you have been notified, have you not?
[PROCTOR *is silent, staring at* ELIZABETH.]
I see light in the sky, Mister; let you counsel with your wife, and may God help you turn your back on Hell.
[PROCTOR *is silent, staring at* ELIZABETH.]

HALE [*quietly*]: Excellency, let –
[DANFORTH *brushes past* HALE *and walks out.* HALE *follows.* CHEEVER *stands and follows,* HATHORNE *behind.* HERRICK *goes.* PARRIS, *from a safe distance, offers*:]

PARRIS: If you desire a cup of cider, Mr Proctor, I am sure I –
[PROCTOR *turns an icy stare at him, and he breaks off.* PARRIS *raises his palms toward* PROCTOR.]
God lead you now. [PARRIS *goes out.*]
[*Alone.* PROCTOR *walks to her, halts. It is as though they stood in a spinning world. It is beyond sorrow, above it. He reaches out his hand as though toward an embodiment not quite real, and as he touches her, a strange soft sound, half laughter, half amazement, comes from his throat. He pats her hand. She covers his hand with hers. And then, weak, he sits. Then she sits, facing him.*]

PROCTOR: The child?

ELIZABETH: It grows.

PROCTOR: There is no word of the boys?

ELIZABETH: They're well. Rebecca's Samuel keeps them.

PROCTOR: You have not seen them?

ELIZABETH: I have not. [*She catches a weakening in herself and downs it.*]

2 **notify sb.**: officially inform sb. 13 **palm**: inside of the hand 16 **spin**: turn quickly arond and around in a circle 17 **embodiment**: (here) sth. that looks like a person but is not real 19 **pat sth.**: touch sth. lightly again and again with your hand (e.g. to comfort sb.) 27 **down sth.**: (here) overcome sth.

PROCTOR: You are a – marvel, Elizabeth.

ELIZABETH: You – have been tortured?

PROCTOR: Aye.
[*Pause. She will not let herself be drowned in the sea that threatens her.*]
They come for my life now.

ELIZABETH: I know it.
[*Pause.*]

PROCTOR: None – have yet confessed?

ELIZABETH: There be many confessed.

PROCTOR: Who are they?

ELIZABETH: There be a hundred or more, they say. Goody Ballard is one; Isaiah Goodkind is one. There be many.

PROCTOR: Rebecca?

ELIZABETH: Not Rebecca. She is one foot in Heaven now; naught may hurt her more.

PROCTOR: And Giles?

ELIZABETH: You have not heard of it?

PROCTOR: I hear nothin', where I am kept.

ELIZABETH: Giles is dead.
[*He looks at her incredulously.*]

PROCTOR: When were he hanged?

ELIZABETH [*quietly, factually*]: He were not hanged. He would not answer aye or nay to his indictment; for if he denied the charge

2 **torture** ['tɔːtʃə(r)]: hurt sb. in order to make them reveal a secret or confess a crime 4 **drown**: *ertrinken* 15 **naught** (old-fashioned) [**nɔːt**]: nothing
23 **factually**: referring to facts, without showing emotion 24 **indictment** [**ɪn'daɪtmənt**]: official accusation

they'd hang him surely, and auction out his property. So he stand mute, and died Christian under the law. And so his sons will have his farm. It is the law, for he could not be condemned a wizard without he answer the indictment, aye or nay.

PROCTOR: Then how does he die?

ELIZABETH [*gently*]: They press him, John.

PROCTOR: Press?

ELIZABETH: Great stones they lay upon his chest until he plead aye or nay. [*With a tender smile for the old man*] They say he give them but two words. 'More weight,' he says. And died.

PROCTOR [*numbed – a thread to weave into his agony*]: 'More weight.'

ELIZABETH: Aye. It were a fearsome man, Giles Corey. [*Pause.*]

PROCTOR [*with great force of will, but not quite looking at her*]: I have been thinking I would confess to them, Elizabeth. [*She shows nothing.*] What say you? If I give them that?

ELIZABETH: I cannot judge you, John.
[*Pause.*]

PROCTOR [*simply – a pure question*]: What would you have me do?

ELIZABETH: As you will, I would have it. [*Slight pause*] I want you living, John. That's sure.

PROCTOR [*pauses, then with a flailing of hope*]: Giles' wife? Have she confessed?

ELIZABETH: She will not.
[*Pause.*]

PROCTOR: It is a pretence, Elizabeth.

1 **auction sth. out**: sell sth. to whoever offers the most money for it 11 **thread**: piece of string used in sewing *(Nähen)* **weave**: make fabric *(Stoff)* from threads **a thread to weave into his agony** (fig.): sth. that makes his suffering worse 12 **fearsome**: (here) inspiring the respect of others 21 **a flailing of hope**: little, newly found hope

ELIZABETH: What is?

PROCTOR: I cannot mount the gibbet like a saint. It is a fraud. I am not that man. [*She is silent.*] My honesty is broke, Elizabeth; I am no good man. Nothing's spoiled by giving them this lie that were not rotten long before.

ELIZABETH: And yet you've not confessed till now. That speak goodness in you.

PROCTOR: Spite only keeps me silent. It is hard to give a lie to dogs. [*Pause, for the first time he turns directly to her.*] I would have your forgiveness, Elizabeth.

ELIZABETH: It is not for me to give, John, I am –

PROCTOR: I'd have you see some honesty in it. Let them that never lied die now to keep their souls. It is pretence for me, a vanity that will not blind God nor keep my children out of the wind. [*Pause.*] What say you?

ELIZABETH [*upon a heaving sob that always threatens*]: John, it come to naught that I should forgive you, if you'll not forgive yourself. [*Now he turns away a little, in great agony.*]
It is not my soul, John, it is yours.
[*He stands, as though in physical pain, slowly rising to his feet with a great immortal longing to find his answer. It is difficult to say, and she is on the verge of tears.*]
Only be sure of this, for I know it now: Whatever you will do, it is a good man does it.
[*He turns his doubting, searching gaze upon her.*]
I have read my heart this three month, John. [*Pause.*] I have sins of my own to count. It needs a cold wife to prompt lechery.

PROCTOR [*in great pain*]: Enough, enough –

8 **spite**: desire to hurt those who have done you wrong 14–15 **keep sb. out of the wind**: keep sb. away from danger 16 **heave**: breathe with great effort 16–17 **come to naught**: be of no use 21 **immortal**: living forever; very intense **longing**: very strong desire 22 **on the verge of tears**: almost crying

ELIZABETH [*now pouring out her heart*]: Better you should know me!

PROCTOR: I will not hear it! I know you!

ELIZABETH: You take my sins upon you, John –

PROCTOR [*in agony*]: No, I take my own, my own!

ELIZABETH: John, I counted myself so plain, so poorly made, no honest love could come to me! Suspicion kissed you when I did; I never knew how I should say my love. It were a cold house I kept! [*In fright, she swerves, as* HATHORNE *enters.*]

HATHORNE: What say you, Proctor? The sun is soon up. [PROCTOR, *his chest heaving, stares, turns to* ELIZABETH. *She comes to him as though to plead, her voice quaking.*]

ELIZABETH: Do what you will. But let none be your judge. There be no higher judge under Heaven than Proctor is! Forgive me, forgive me, John – I never knew such goodness in the world! [*She covers her face, weeping.*]

[PROCTOR *turns from her to* HATHORNE; *he is off the earth, his voice hollow.*]

PROCTOR: I want my life.

HATHORNE [*electrified, surprised*]: You'll confess yourself?

PROCTOR: I will have my life.

HATHORNE [*with a mystical tone*]: God be praised! It is a providence! [*He rushes out the door, and his voice is heard calling down the corridor:*] He will confess! Proctor will confess!

PROCTOR [*with a cry, as he strides to the door*]: Why do you cry it? [*In great pain he turns back to her.*] It is evil, is it not? It is evil.

ELIZABETH [*in terror, weeping*]: I cannot judge you, John, I cannot!

5 **plain**: (here) not pretty or attractive 8 **swerve**: make a sudden movement to one side 19 **electrify sb.**: make sb. feel excited

PROCTOR: Then who will judge me? [*Suddenly clasping his hands*] God in Heaven, what is John Proctor, what is John Proctor? [*He moves as an animal, and a fury is riding in him, a tantalized search.*] I think it is honest, I think so; I am no saint. [*As though she had denied this he calls angrily at her*] Let Rebecca go like a saint; for me it is fraud!
[*Voices are heard in the hall, speaking together in suppressed excitement.*]

ELIZABETH: I am not your judge, I cannot be. [*As though giving him release*] Do as you will, do as you will!

PROCTOR: Would you give them such a lie? Say it. Would you ever give them this? [*She cannot answer.*] You would not; if tongs of fire were singeing you you would not! It is evil. Good, then – it is evil, and I do it!
[HATHORNE *enters with* DANFORTH, *and, with them*, CHEEVER, PARRIS, *and* HALE. *It is a businesslike, rapid entrance, as though the ice had been broken.*]

DANFORTH [*with great relief and gratitude*]: Praise to God, man, praise to God; you shall be blessed in Heaven for this.
[CHEEVER *has hurried to the bench with pen, ink, and paper.* PROCTOR *watches him.*]
Now then, let us have it. Are you ready, Mr Cheever?

PROCTOR [*with a cold, cold horror at their efficiency*]: Why must it be written?

DANFORTH: Why, for the good instruction of the village, Mister; this we shall post upon the church door! [*To* PARRIS, *urgently*] Where is the marshal?

3 **tantalized**: suffering greatly because you cannot have sth. you want very much
7 **suppress sth.**: trying not to show sth. (e.g. feelings) 9–10 **give sb. release**: make sb. free (e.g. from guilt) 12 **tongs**: *Zange* 13 **singe sb./sth. [sɪndʒ]**: burn sb./sth. 16–17 **the ice had been broken**: the first step had been taken
25 **instruction**: (here) teaching 26 **post sth.**: make sth. known by hanging a piece of writing in a public place

PARRIS [*runs to the door and calls down the corridor*]: Marshal! Hurry!

DANFORTH: Now, then, Mister, will you speak slowly, and directly to the point, for Mr Cheever's sake. [*He is on record now, and is really dictating to* CHEEVER, *who writes.*] Mr Proctor, have you seen the Devil in your life? [PROCTORS'S *jaws lock.*] Come, man, there is light in the sky; the town waits at the scaffold; I would give out this news. Did you see the Devil?

PROCTOR: I did.

PARRIS: Praise God!

DANFORTH: And when he come to you, what were his demand? [PROCTOR *is silent.* DANFORTH *helps.*] Did he bid you to do his work upon the earth?

PROCTOR: He did.

DANFORTH: And you bound yourself to his service? [DANFORTH *turns, as* REBECCA NURSE *enters, with* HERRICK *helping to support her. She is barely able to walk.*] Come in, come in, woman!

REBECCA [*brightening as she sees* PROCTOR]: Ah, John! You are well, then, eh?
[PROCTOR *turns his face to the wall.*]

DANFORTH: Courage, man, courage – let her witness your good example that she may come to God herself. Now hear it, Goody Nurse! Say on, Mr Proctor. Did you bind yourself to the Devil's service?

REBECCA [*astonished*]: Why, John!

PROCTOR [*through his teeth, his face turned from* REBECCA]: I did.

DANFORTH: Now, woman, you surely see it profit nothin' to keep this conspiracy any further. Will you confess yourself with him?

3 **be on record**: (here) have written proof of what you say 5 **(Proctor's) jaws lock**: (Proctor) presses his teeth together tightly 6 **scaffold**: platform on which people are executed

REBECCA: Oh, John – God send his mercy on you!

DANFORTH: I say, will you confess yourself, Goody Nurse?

REBECCA: Why, it is a lie, it is a lie; how may I damn myself? I cannot, I cannot.

DANFORTH: Mr Proctor. When the Devil came to you did you see Rebecca Nurse in his company? [PROCTOR *is silent.*] Come, man, take courage – did you ever see her with the Devil?

PROCTOR [*almost inaudibly*]: No.
[DANFORTH, *now sensing trouble, glances at* JOHN *and goes to the table, and picks up a sheet – the list of condemned.*]

DANFORTH: Did you ever see her sister, Mary Easty, with the Devil?

PROCTOR: No, I did not.

DANFORTH [*his eyes narrow on* PROCTOR:] Did you ever see Martha Corey with the Devil?

PROCTOR: I did not.

DANFORTH [*realizing, slowly putting the sheet down*]: Did you ever see anyone with the Devil?

PROCTOR: I did not.

DANFORTH: Proctor, you mistake me. I am not empowered to trade your life for a lie. You have most certainly seen some person with the Devil. [PROCTOR *is silent.*] Mr Proctor, a score of people have already testified they saw this woman with the Devil.

PROCTOR: Then it is proved. Why must I say it?

DANFORTH: Why 'must you' say it! Why, you should rejoice to say it if your soul is truly purged of any love for Hell!

PROCTOR: They think to go like saints. I like not to spoil their names.

19 **trade sth. for sth.**: give sth. to a person who gives you sth. in return 21 **score**: (here) twenty 24 **rejoice**: show that you are happy 25 **purge**: make clean

DANFORTH [*inquiring, incredulous*]: Mr Proctor, do you think they go like saints?

PROCTOR [*evading*]: This woman never thought she done the Devil's work.

DANFORTH: Look you, sir. I think you mistake your duty here. It matters nothing what she thought – she is convicted of the unnatural murder of children, and you for sending your spirit out upon Mary Warren. Your soul alone is the issue here, Mister, and you will prove its whiteness or you cannot live in a Christian country. Will you tell me now what persons conspired with you in the Devil's company? [PROCTOR *is silent.*] To your knowledge was Rebecca Nurse ever –

PROCTOR: I speak my own sins; I cannot judge another. [*Crying out, with hatred*] I have no tongue for it.

HALE [*quickly to* DANFORTH]: Excellency, it is enough he confess himself. Let him sign it, let him sign it.

PARRIS [*feverishly*]: It is a great service, sir. It is a weighty name; it will strike the village that Proctor confess. I beg you, let him sign it. The sun is up, Excellency!

DANFORTH [*considers; then with dissatisfaction*]: Come, then, sign your testimony. [*To* CHEEVER] Give it to him. [CHEEVER *goes to* PROCTOR, *the confession and a pen in hand.* PROCTOR *does not look at it.*]
Come, man, sign it.

PROCTOR [*after glancing at the confession*]: You have all witnessed it – it is enough.

DANFORTH: You will not sign it?

PROCTOR: You have all witnessed it; what more is needed?

2 **convict sb. of sth.**: decide in court that sb. has done sth. (a crime) and will be punished for it 10 **conspire with sb.**: make secret plans with sb. (e.g. to do sth. illegal) 17 **weighty**: important

DANFORTH: Do you sport with me? You will sign your name or it is no confession, Mister! [*His breast heaving with agonized breathing,* PROCTOR *now lays the paper down and signs his name.*]

PARRIS: Praise be to the Lord!
[PROCTOR *has just finished signing when* DANFORTH *reaches for the paper. But* PROCTOR *snatches it up, and now a wild terror is rising in him, and a boundless anger.*]

DANFORTH [*perplexed, but politely extending his hand*]: If you please, sir.

PROCTOR: No.

DANFORTH [*as though* PROCTOR *did not understand*]: Mr Proctor, I must have –

PROCTOR: No, no. I have signed it. You have seen me. It is done! You have no need for this.

PARRIS: Proctor, the village must have proof that –

PROCTOR: Damn the village! I confess to God, and God has seen my name on this! It is enough!

DANFORTH: No, sir, it is –

PROCTOR: You came to save my soul, did you not? Here! I have confessed myself; it is enough!

DANFORTH: You have not con –

PROCTOR: I have confessed myself! Is there no good penitence but it be public? God does not need my name nailed upon the church! God sees my name; God knows how black my sins are! It is enough!

DANFORTH: Mr Proctor –

7 **boundless**: without limit or end; extreme 8 **extend a hand**: reach out with your hand 22 **penitence**: state of being sorry for sth. bad you have done

PROCTOR: You will not use me! I am no Sarah Good or Tituba, I am John Proctor! You will not use me! It is no part of salvation that you should use me!

DANFORTH: I do not wish to –

PROCTOR: I have three children – how may I teach them to walk like men in the world, and I sold my friends?

DANFORTH: You have not sold your friends –

PROCTOR: Beguile me not! I blacken all of them when this is nailed to the church the very day they hang for silence!

DANFORTH: Mr Proctor, I must have good and legal proof that you –

PROCTOR: You are the high court, your word is good enough! Tell them I confessed myself; say Proctor broke his knees and wept like a woman; say what you will, but my name cannot –

DANFORTH [*with suspicion*]: It is the same, is it not? If I report it or you sign to it?

PROCTOR [*he knows it is insane*]: No, it is not the same! What others say and what I sign to is not the same!

DANFORTH: Why? Do you mean to deny this confession when you are free?

PROCTOR: I mean to deny nothing!

DANFORTH: Then explain to me, Mr Proctor, why you will not let –

PROCTOR [*with a cry of his soul*]: Because it is my name! Because I cannot have another in my life! Because I lie and sign myself to lies! Because I am not worth the dust on the feet of them that hang! How may I live without my name? I have given you my soul; leave me my name!

2 **salvation**: being saved in a religious sense

DANFORTH [*pointing at the confession in Proctor's hand*]: Is that document a lie? If it is a lie I will not accept it! What say you? I will not deal in lies, Mister! [PROCTOR *is motionless.*] You will give me your honest confession in my hand, or I cannot keep you from the rope. [PROCTOR *does not reply.*] Which way do you go, Mister? [*His breast heaving, his eyes staring,* PROCTOR *tears the paper and crumples it, and he is weeping in fury, but erect.*]Marshal!

PARRIS [*hysterically, as though the tearing paper were his life*]: Proctor, Proctor!

HALE: Man, you will hang! You cannot!

PROCTOR [*his eyes full of tears*]: I can. And there's your first marvel, that I can. You have made your magic now, for now I do think I see some shred of goodness in John Proctor. Not enough to weave a banner with, but white enough to keep it from such dogs. [ELIZABETH, *in a burst of terror, rushes to him and weeps against his hand.*]
Give them no tear! Tears pleasure them! Show honour now, show a stony heart and sink them with it! [*He has lifted her, and kisses her now with great passion.*]

REBECCA: Let you fear nothing! Another judgement waits us all!

DANFORTH: Hang them high over the town! Who weeps for these, weeps for corruption! [*He sweeps out past them.* HERRICK *starts to lead* REBECCA, *who almost collapses, but* PROCTOR *catches her, and she glances up at him apologetically.*]

REBECCA: I've had no breakfast.

HERRICK: Come, man.
[HERRICK *escorts them out,* HATHORNE *and* CHEEVER *behind them.* ELIZABETH *stands staring at the empty doorway.*]

3 **motionless**: not moving 13 **shred of sth.**: small piece of sth. 13–14 **not enough to weave a banner with** (fig.): not very much at all 15 **burst**: sudden, short moment 22 **sweep**: walk quickly and with determination 27 **escort sb.**: walk along with sb.

PARRIS [*in deadly fear, to* ELIZABETH]: Go to him, Goody Proctor! There is yet time!
[*From outside a drumroll strikes the air.* PARRIS *is startled.* ELIZABETH *jerks about toward the window.*]

PARRIS: Go to him! [*He rushes out the door, as though to hold back his fate.*] Proctor! Proctor!
[*Again, a short burst of drums.*]

HALE: Woman, plead with him! [*He starts to rush out the door, and then goes back to her.*] Woman! It is pride, it is vanity. [*She avoids his eyes, and moves to the window. He drops to his knees.*]
Be his helper! – What profit him to bleed? Shall the dust praise him? Shall the worms declare his truth? Go to him, take his shame away!

ELIZABETH [*supporting herself against collapse, grips the bars of the window, and with a cry*]: He have his goodness now. God forbid I take it from him!
[*The final drumroll crashes, then heightens violently.* HALE *weeps in frantic prayer, and the new sun is pouring in upon her face, and the drums rattle like bones in the morning air.*]

THE CURTAIN FALLS

3 **drumroll**: fast series of drum beats, usually to show that sth. important is about to happen 17 **heighten** ['haɪtn]: (here) get stronger

ADDTIONAL MATERIALS

Echoes down the corridor

Not long after the fever died, Parris was voted from office, walked out on the highroad, and was never heard of again.

The legend has it that Abigail turned up later as a prostitute in Boston.

Twenty years after the last execution, the government awarded compensation to the victims still living, and to the families of the dead. However, it is evident that some people still were unwilling to admit their total guilt, and also that the factionalism was still alive, for some beneficiaries were actually not victims at all, but informers.

Elizabeth Proctor married again, four years after Proctor's death.

In solemn meeting, the congregation rescinded the excommunications – this in March 1712. But they did so upon orders of the government. The jury, however, wrote a statement praying forgiveness of all who had suffered.

Certain farms which had belonged to the victims were left to ruin, and for more than a century no one would buy them or live on them.

To all intents and purposes, the power of theocracy in Massachusetts was broken.

by Arthur Miller

6 **compensation**: money given to people who have had to suffer injustice
8 **factionalism**: (here) division of the population into groups with different opinions 9 **beneficiary** [ˌbenɪˈfɪʃəri]: person who profits from sth., usually by being given money 11 **rescind sth.** [rɪˈsɪnd]: declare that sth. is no longer valid (usu. a law, decision etc.) 18 **to all intents and purposes**: almost completely

Salem witch trials

The Salem witch trials occurred between February 1692 and May 1693. During that time, more than 200 people were accused of witchcraft: 19 were hanged, one was pressed to death with a heavy stone and seven died in prison. The trials occurred throughout several towns in the province, including Ipswich, Andover, Salem Village and Salem Town.

In January 1692, the daughter and niece of Reverend Samuel Parris became ill. They had unusual symptoms: they screamed that their skin was being pinched and poked, they barked and made unusual sounds, and they threw things. A doctor, William Griggs, was called in to help, but couldn't find a cure. He concluded that the girls were possessed by the Devil. Soon afterwards, other girls in Salem began to show similar symptoms.

In late February, the town magistrates pressured the girls to reveal the source of their afflictions. They accused Tituba, the Parris' slave, Sarah Good, a homeless beggar, and Sarah Osborne, a poor, elderly woman. All of these women were town misfits, and therefore no one defended them. Good and Osborne pleaded not guilty, however Tituba admitted that the Devil had come to her and she had signed her name in his book. All three women were put into jail.

Over the following months, several more accusations followed. By the end of May 1692, 62 people were held in custody, accused of witchcraft. On June 2, 1692, the Court of Oyer and Terminer assembled and tried their first case: Bridget Bishop. She was found guilty and eight days later, she was the first of the accused to be hanged. By October 1692, thirteen women and five men suffered similar fates.

9 **pinch**: *klemmen* 9 **bark**: make the sound of a dog 11 **conclude**: reach a decision 15 **affliction**: pain or suffering 17 **misfit**: person who doesn't fit into society

In October, the Court of Oyer and Terminer was disbanded. Governor Phipps, whose own wife was being questioned about witchcraft, stopped the proceedings of the court largely because they had been basing their judgments on spectral evidence. Spectral evidence (testimony that individuals took on invisible shapes in dreams and visions to torture victims) was later ruled unlawful.

The Superior Court of Judicature took over from the Court of Oyer and Terminer. It did not allow spectral evidence and found only 3 out of 56 defendants guilty of witchcraft. By May 1693, Phipps pardoned all who were in prison; in effect, the Salem witch trials were over. However it could not undo the damage that had already been done.

In 1702, the General Court declared the witch trials unlawful. Nine years later, the colony restored the good names of all those accused and gave £600 to their heirs as compensation. Finally in 1957, the state of Massachusetts officially apologized for the events.

In more recent years, research has been done to uncover the cause of the mass hysteria in Salem. In 1976, one historian suggested that natural hallucinogen Ergot could have been the source of the girls' strange behavior: this poison attacks the central nervous system, causing mania, insanity, visions, tingling sensations and paralysis. It grows on wheat and could easily have been in the flour used to make bread in Salem.

by Ralph Williams and Christine Finke

1 **disband sth.**: break sth. up (e.g. a group or organisation) 10 **pardon sb.**: forgive sb. 15 **heir**: person who gets your money after you die 15 **compensation**: money given to you because of suffering or damages you endured in the past
21 **insanity**: *Irrsinn* **tingle**: *kribbeln* 22 **wheat**: *Weize* **flour**: *Mehl*

Hollywood Blacklist

In the 1930s and '40s, while Americans were suffering the effects of World War II and the Great Depression (and long before the true horrors of Stalin's rule in Russia were known to the West), the American Communist Party attracted many followers. Many of them were young, left-wing idealists working in the arts and entertainment industries. The American Communist Party fought for the rights of poor people in the U.S. and was very important in securing unemployment, disability and social security benefits for the American people. To be a Communist in 1930s America did not carry the same stigma it does today.

After Word War II, American suspicion turned away from Japan and Nazi Germany towards Communist Russia. In October 1947, the House Committee of Un-American Activities used a list of alleged Communist sympathizers, published by *The Hollywood Reporter*, to summon people working in the film industry for investigation. At the beginning of their hearings, a few big names (including Walt Disney and Ronald Reagan) testified that Communists in the film industry were a threat to national security. As the media began extensive coverage of the proceedings, a group of allegedly communist writers, producers and directors were nicknamed the "Hollywood Ten".

The "Ten" consisted of Alvah Bessie, Herbert Biberman, Lester Cole, Edward Dmytryk, Ring Lardner, Jr., John Howard Lawson, Albert Maltz, Sam Ornitz, Robert Adrian Scott, and Dalton Trumbo. All were jailed for up to one year each, fined $1,000 and "blacklisted". With their names on the blacklist, they were effectively banned from finding work in Hollywood.

5 **left-wing**: with political ideas that money, power and property should be shared more equally in society 11 **suspicion**: feeling that you can't trust people 13 **alleged**: *angeblich* 14 **sympathizer**: person who supports or approves of a particular political party 16 **hearing**: trial 17 **testify**: make a statement in court

Although the House Committee of Un-American Activities failed to find any real evidence that Hollywood was secretly producing Communist propaganda, the witch hunt was far from over. In September 1950, Edward Dmytryk (a well-known director and one of the "Hollywood Ten") publicly admitted that he had been a Communist in his past and that he was willing to give evidence against other Communists. He was released early from jail, and the film industry descended into a riot of finger-pointing and reputation-smearing. People were desperate to avoid being blacklisted; they accused others of supporting Communism to divert attention from themselves. In 1951, a second investigation into connections between Hollywood and Communism began.

At the height of the blacklisting period between 1952 and 1956, over 500 individuals were accused of Communist-affiliations and found themselves unemployable. The FBI tapped peoples' phones, opened their post and placed them under continuous surveillance. The atmosphere in Hollywood was so guarded and tense, that this once liberal mecca showed little support for pressing issues of the day, such as African-American civil rights and opposition to nuclear testing.

In 1962, disgraced radio-presenter John Henry Faulk won a landmark lawsuit and brought the witch hunt to an end. He had been fired from his job at CBS radio in 1957 for alleged Communist sympathies, and had decided to sue those responsible for his dismissal. The court decision meant that people could legally claim for professional and financial losses they had suffered from being blacklisted. This move put an end to blacklisting and allowed many to return to work and restore their reputations. Despite this good news, many professionals felt bitter towards those who had effectively ruined their careers by accusing them. Others, who had

8 **smear sb./sth.**: (here) say bad things about sb./sth. 10 **divert sth.**: make sth. change direction 14 **affiliation**: (here) connection 16 **surveillance**: *Beobachtung* 17 **guarded**: very careful 18 **mecca**: (here) centre **pressing**: (here) important 21 **disgraced**: with a bad reputation

buckled under pressure and blackened the names of friends and coworkers, felt guilty. In 1963, actor Sterling Hayden said, "I was a rat, a stoolie, and the names I named of those close friends were blacklisted and deprived of their livelihood."

by Ralph Williams and Christine Finke

1 **buckle**: become weak 3 **stoolie** (sl): person who gives secret information in return for money or protection

McCarthyism

The term “McCarthyism” was first coined during a period after World War II in the United States called the “Second Red Scare”. At that time, there was a heightened fear and suspicion of communism. Republican Senator Joseph McCarthy, after whom the term is named, used the tense atmosphere in America to his advantage in an effort to boost his popularity. Fearing that he would not be re-elected in 1950, he gave a campaign speech on February 12th of that year, claiming to have a list with the names of 205 people in the government who were communists. With the help of these claims, McCarthy was re-elected and became a member of the House Un-American Activities Committee.

With the Cold War underway and communist governments in eastern Europe and China, McCarthy's attacks on government leaders and movie stars helped feed the hysteria in America. Soon after, he became the chairman of the Senate Committee on Government Operations. McCarthy was allowed to investigate suspects more thoroughly, and hundreds of witnesses were put on the stand in front of the Senate committee. McCarthy's interview methods were very intimidating and he often used the threat of jail to get more information. Americans turned on their fellow citizens, making claims based on little or no proof in order to take the spotlight off themselves. Many reputations were ruined and many lost their jobs as the names of suspected communists were released to the public.

Additionally, McCarthy suspected that many Hollywood figures, including actors, screenwriters, producers and directors had communist ties. An ‘entertainment industry blacklist’ was created and those on the list were not able to get jobs. The first ten people questioned by McCarthy were called ‘the Hollywood Ten’. They

1 **coin sth.**: create sth. new (e.g. a phrase) 6 **boost sth.**: (here) make sth. stronger 12 **underway**: having already started 19 **intimidating**: frightening 20 **turn on sb.**: attack sb. 25 **screenwriter**: person who writes scripts for films and television

chose not to cooperate with McCarthy, citing their right to free speech in the First Amendment. This resulted in eight of the ten individuals being sent to prison for one year and two of them for six months. All of the members of the Hollywood Ten were also fired from their jobs. Arthur Miller, author of the 'The Crucible', was another famous figure who was found guilty of being a communist. However, his verdict was overturned in 1957.

McCarthy began to lose support after he was shown on television in 1954, interviewing major figures in the United States Army. When they didn't answer questions as McCarthy desired, he told them they were a disgrace and not fit to wear their uniforms. The public did not appreciate McCarthy insulting the Armed Forces and opinions quickly shifted.

That same year, the Senate charged McCarthy for abuse of power as a senator. He was allowed to remain in office, but had very little influence. Three years later, McCarthy died at the age of 48 of acute hepatitis, caused by alcoholism.

In today's context, "McCarthyism" can describe the general practice of making unfair accusations without real supporting evidence. It has become synonymous with witch hunts, sham trials and mass hysteria. Ironically, years later it was found out that many of the individuals accused by McCarthy did indeed have communist ties.

11 **not fit to do sth.**: not good enough to do sth. 13 **shift**: change dramatically
20 **sham**: fake

Mass Hysteria In Upstate New York

Last August, 16-year-old Lori Brownell passed out while head-banging at a concert. A month later, she lost consciousness again at her school's homecoming dance in upstate Corinth, N.Y. Brownell says her doctors put her on Celexa, but she only developed more symptoms, including involuntary twitching and clapping. In videos she posted to YouTube, Brownell flutters her fingers, touches her hair, snorts through her nose and throat, and shouts "Hey, hey, hey," seemingly without control. On Christmas Eve, doctors diagnosed her with Tourette's Syndrome. Now, however, her symptoms have another name: conversion disorder, or mass hysteria.

Since Brownell first passed out last summer, 14 other upstate New York students –13 girls and a boy, most of them students at LeRoy Junior-Senior High School – have come down with similar symptoms. The young people and their parents seem baffled. The state department of health and a separate report commissioned by the school have found no problematic substances in the building. […]

However, a doctor treating many of the students is confident that they are suffering not from poisoning, but from mass hysteria, also called mass psychogenic illness and other variants. Typically, symptoms – which can include Brownell's Tourette's-like movements, along with nausea, dizziness, cramping, and more – start with one or two victims and spread when others see or hear about them. Victims are often accused of faking it, but more often they are suffering real physical symptoms that are psychological in origin. The phenomenon has been observed for centuries, with the blame shifting to whatever specific anxieties are culturally pervasive at the time. But one theme has remained consistent: The victims are overwhelmingly female.

1 **pass out**: faint; become unconscious 4 **Celexa**: drug used to treat depression 5 **involuntary**: happening without you wanting it 6 **flutter**: move lightly and quickly 14 **baffled**: totally confused 26 **pervasive**: existing 27–28 **overwhelmingly**: mostly

The most famous American incident of mass hysteria remains the events surrounding the witch trials in Salem, Mass., which began when several girls began suffering mysterious fits and outbursts. In non-Western countries, demons and witchcraft are still sometimes blamed for outbreaks of fainting and fits. Pollution, poisoning, chemical weapons, and other environmental concerns are dominant in the West [...] Some bloggers are now claiming that the upstate New York girls fell ill because of the HPV vaccine or fracking.

As archetypes go, the Salem events hold up quite well, even from a distance of 320 years. Victims of mass hysteria are so often female that gender imbalance is one clue doctors use to differentiate hysteria from poisoning. Symptoms often start with older girls or women and spread to younger or lower-status girls. As girlhood guardian Caitlin Flanagan put it in the New York Times this weekend, "It is the cheerleaders and not the linebackers who come down with tics and stuttering." But, as research has shown, it is also the cheerleaders and not the math-club girls who are likely to spread hysteria.

In a typical case in 1998, a teacher at a Tennessee high school noticed a gas-like odor in her classroom. The school was quickly evacuated, but the teacher's symptoms spread to more than 180 teachers and students, who exhibited symptoms including headaches, nausea, and vomiting. By the end of the ordeal, the school had to be closed for two weeks and almost $100,000 was spent on emergency medical care. No toxins were ever found. A later study of the incident in the New England Journal of Medicine – one of surprisingly few on the phenomenon of mass hysteria – found that symptoms were "significantly associated with female sex, seeing another ill person, knowing that a classmate was ill, and reporting an unusual odor at the school."

3 **outburst**: sudden, strong expression or emotion 8 **HPV vaccine**: *HPV Impfung* **fracking**: technique of getting gas, oil or gas out of the earth 15 **tic**: *nervöser Krampf* 19 **odor** (AE): smell

There's no consensus about why women and girls are more vulnerable to episodes of mass hysteria. One professor speculated last year that "Stress, boredom, concern about their children and other factors among young females" could have triggered a recent fainting epidemic among female factory workers in Cambodia. Sociologist Robert Bartholomew noted in a 2001 book on mass hysteria that girls are trained to turn their anxieties inward, while anxious boys are likelier to act out. Women are also likelier to seek medical treatment than men.

Some scholars have also argued that hysterical episodes allow women to take a break from daily drudgeries, or to rage against patriarchal cultures within the safe bounds of demon possession or poisoning. If girls can find no outlet for reckless abandon, in other words, they'll create one. Barbara Ehrenreich, Elizabeth Hess, and Gloria Jacobs put it this way in a 1992 essay: "To abandon control – to scream, faint, dash about in mobs – was, in form if not in conscious intent, to protest the sexual repressiveness, the rigid double standard of female teen culture." They were writing about Beatlemania, as it turns out, but the description of the wildness that overcomes girls in adolescence is almost identical to much scholarly musing about mass hysteria.

There is also, it must be noted, a long history of medical professionals dismissing women's health concerns as mere hysteria. This makes treatment thorny. Sufferers naturally want to be taken seriously, and are often offended by suggestions that their symptoms are "all in their heads." Several of the upstate New York victims and their families told the Today show that they're not satisfied with the new diagnosis. "Obviously all of us are not accepting that this is just a stress thing, and our kids didn't all get sick by coincidence," one father said. A few cases diagnosed as mass hysteria at the time have

1 **consensus**: agreement 2 **speculate**: guess 8 **act out** (sl): behave badly
11 **drudgery**: boring occupation 13 **reckless abandon**: enjoyment without responsibilities 24 **thorny**: (here) problematic

later proved to be poisoning after all; a 1990 outbreak of nausea at a British school that affected girls at almost twice the rate of boys turned out to be largely explained by pesticides used on cucumbers served at lunch. But almost always, symptoms disappear on their own over time and no physical causes are discovered.

Until more is known about mass hysteria, the treatment of a 1789 case in Northern England might point the way to a cure both effective and enjoyable. The outbreak at a textile factory started when one woman teased another by putting a mouse in her dress; the skittish prank victim fell into convulsions. Soon, however, a rumor spread that an open bag of imported cotton had somehow caused the reaction, and others quickly began falling ill. The factory had to temporarily shut down when 24 people (21 women, two young girls, and one man) experienced violent convulsions so severe they had to be restrained. The plague ended when authorities convinced the patients that symptoms were "merely nervous." To further tamp down anxieties, sufferers were encouraged to "take a cheerful glass and join in a dance." The day after the dance, almost all the victims went back to work, their convulsions having disappeared for good.

01/31/2012, by Ruth Graham, *Huffington Post*

11 **skittish**: nervous **convulsion**: sudden, uncontrollable shaking of the body
18 **tamp sth. down**: make sth. less extreme 18–19 **take a glass**: have (here) have an alcoholic drink

THE AUTHOR

Arthur Miller was born in New York in 1915 and studied at the University of Michigan. His plays include *All My Sons* (1947); *Death of a Salesman* (1949), which won the Pulitzer Prize and the Drama Critics's Circle Award; *The Crucible* (1953), which won a Tony Award; *A Memory of Two Mondays* (1955); *A View from the Bridge* (1955); *After the Fall* (1963); *Incident at Vichy* (1964); *The Price* (1968); *The Archbishop's Ceiling* (1977); *The American Clock* (1980); *Playing for Time* (1981), which won the Peabody Award; *Two-Way Mirror* (1985); *Danger: Memory!* (1986); *Ride Down Mount Morgan* (1990); *The Last Yankee* (1992); and *Broken Glass* (1994), which won the Olivier Award for Best Play in 1995. His play *The Creation of the World and Other Business* (1972) was made into a musical, *Up From Paradise*, in 1974. His screenplay for film include *The Misfits*, starring Clark Gable and Marilyn Monroe; and *The Crucible*, starring Daniel Day Lewis, Winona Ryder and Paul Scofield, which was nominated for an American Award for Best Screenplay in 1996.

Arthur Miller has been awarded Honorary Doctorates from Harvard and Oxford Universities. In addition to his works for stage and screen he is also the author of *Focus*, a novel; *I Don't Need You Anymore*, a collection of short stories; and *Plain Girl*, a short work of prose fiction. In collaboration with his wife, the photographer Inge Morath, he has published *In Russia* (1969); *In the Country* (1977); *Chinese Encounters* (1979); and *Salesman in Beijing* (1984), based on his experience directing a production of *Death of a Salesman* in China. His autobiography, *Time Bends*, was published in 1987.